$9.95

D0880933

Freedom and Capital

MAINSTREAM SERIES

Editors: Lord Blake, Leon Brittan, Jo Grimond, John Patten and Alan Peacock

DAVID HOWELL

Freedom and Capital

Prospects for the
Property-Owning Democracy

BASIL BLACKWELL · OXFORD

First published 1981 by
Basil Blackwell Publisher
108 Cowley Road
Oxford OX4 1JF
England

British Library Cataloguing in Publication Data

Howell, David, b.1936
    Freedom and capital. – (Mainstream series)
    1. Great Britain – Politics and government
    I. Title   II. Series
    320.9'41'0857   JN234

    ISBN 0-631-12552-3

Typesetting by Getset (BTS) Ltd, Eynsham, Oxford
Printed in Great Britain by Book Plan, Worcester

CONTENTS

For Davina

FOREWORD

These reflections on the political debate in Britain in the 1970s — although revised for final publication — were substantially written before the decade was out, and before the Conservative Government took office in May 1979. They are therefore in no sense a statement of the present Government's views, or part of a collective voice. The book is an entirely personal assessment which looks back into the seventies and tries to draw some lessons for policy makers from those years.

Its publication now is apt for three reasons. First, recovery is coming, but the recession has been deep. The oil crisis has made it deeper and the process of adjustment for Britain, with its old industrial structure set side by side with its new North Sea oil and gas, has proved especially painful. This is all the more reason for ensuring that *this time*, as economic confidence flows back, we avoid repeating the terrible mistakes of the past.

Second, despite the new mood of realism in our country, the lessons of the seventies still seem very far from fully learned in some quarters. The confusion between the old middle way which led nowhere, and the new common ground which politicians should now be seeking still persists. It seemed to me, reading this manuscript eighteen months or more after it was written, that the challenge it offered to that confusion and all the muddle and myth and false analysis that went with it, is just as much worth making as ever.

Third, my colleagues have been kind enough to encourage me to let this essay be published. All authors like encouragement: so here it is.

D.H.

CHAPTER 1

Introduction

> Nowadays there does seem to be a gradual convergence
> of reasonable men towards a scientifically studied and
> planned socialism.
>> H. G. Wells *A Short History of the World*

Two purposes were originally in my mind when I started to
write this book. The first was to try and combat what might
be called the 'irreversibility' thesis, the widespread and
defeatist view, which seemed to reach its zenith in Britain in
the late 1970s, that the continuing growth of state and trade
union power was inevitable, that personal freedoms were
bound to go on shrinking under the evolutionary advance of
collectivism and social ownership, and that the best that
'realists' and 'men of goodwill' could do was to try and
temper the pace of this development by a tactical mixture of
appeasement and firmness. By contrast I wanted to try and
show that there were already new forces and pressures at
work which were pushing British society in a totally different
direction — not necessarily back towards a pre-socialist
capitalist system, if ever such a thing really existed, but
forward towards a much more open, less class-categorized
kind of community, with a far wider diffusion of power, and
therefore a far greater claim to be genuinely democratic than
anything achieved by the egalitarian zeal of recent decades.

My second purpose was to argue for changed attitudes amongst politicians and policy-makers — and for changed policies in consequence — which would allow these new impulses in British society to grow, rather than smother them. In particular, I wanted to resurrect the strangely neglected theme of broadened personal ownership as a means of helping a post-socialist society into being, of further undermining the myth of the alleged 'conflict' between labour and capital and of offering firmer common ground for the future than the consensus policies of the sixties could provide.

Since I began to think about these ideas events have undoubtedly helped make it steadily easier for me to formulate my case. I do not believe it would be an exaggeration to say that socialism in Britain is now on the defensive, and not just in party political terms, but in intellectual terms as well. For the first time in years, opponents of the collectivist philosophy have begun to shed some of the moral inferiority, the almost apologetic quality which has so characterized post-war non-socialist politics. People in public discussion and debate have begun, as Lord Hailsham puts it, to find themselves increasingly compelled 'to use arguments founded on the half-forgotten conceptions of right and wrong, justice and injustice'.[1] The march of ideology has faltered.

Nor is it difficult to see why this new situation should have come about. Socialism in Britain was supposed to be going to bring a new sense of fairness and unity, healing the divisions of the bad past. But if we take one of the main planks of Labour Party policy, so-called 'public ownership', we find no trace in it at all of any fresh sense of fairness or justice or unity. On the contrary, the process has created new elites, new divisions and new grievances. Or if we look at the great centrepieces of the post-war welfare state, the health service, the education service, the social services, we find much sincere and dedicated effort long since discredited by soulless bureaucratic agencies and over-centralization, a prospect about which Anthony Crosland was concerned just before he died.[2]

As for the belief that taxation could be an instrument for spreading wealth and increasing social cohesion, this, too, has turned sour. With the average manual worker paying a quarter of his wages in tax, redistributive 'justice' has turned out to be a vast gyratory fraud, a source not of growing contentment but of immense bitterness and frustration, nowhere more so than between those who work and pay heavy tax on modest wages and those who are not at work, draw benefits and pay no income tax on them.

None of this of course is intended to suggest for one moment that the battle against collectivist simplicities is won − indeed it has hardly begun. All this record of undeniable failure means is that claims for the 'inevitability' of socialism in Britain, which seemed at one time to paralyse creative political thought amongst socialists and non-socialists alike, no longer look anything like so convincing. It reminds us that there is, after all, a choice of direction which it is within our power to make, and that at the end of a very long and very dark tunnel, from which it is going to take some while to emerge, one can just see a faint glimmer of light.

Nor, when a once-binding faith collapses − and British socialism in its heyday certainly had that quality − is it necessarily a time, even for those who fought against that faith, to stand and cheer unreservedly. Amidst a shower of broken hopes, smashed loyalties and unbrotherly recrimination, a dangerous vacuum opens up. The question then arises, 'What will hold our society and our nation together?' 'Where will the new common ground be established, upon which a people who are casting aside the old social moulds can again find unity and some degree of shared purpose?'

We need look no further than the crime figures, and perhaps even more the spread of aimless, motiveless violent behaviour amongst younger people, to realize the extraordinary urgency of these questions. Lawlessness and vandalism on the scale they have now reached in Britain are unmistakeable signs of social disintegration. And so too, I think most people would agree, are the furies of the picket line, vandals no less, who have no time for union authority or union codes of behaviour and who are prepared to use anybody, however sick, however old, however vulnerable, in their frenzied drive to get what they want and must immediately have.

Of course it is entirely right to say that these dangers must be met by the restoration of the rule of law. The law, after all, is the bond which holds a civilized community together, which allows people to live and go about their business with some degree of security. But the law, too, relies on a wide degree of consent and acceptance, both in its making and its enforcement. Unless people feel that they are part of the society which the law serves and supports, the cement will not hold.

It must be right, too, that much less dominance by the state, and a general return to social organization on a more human scale, in a way that enlarges personal choice and links personal responsibility more closely to effort, will help greatly to reduce the divisions in our society and, by softening the 'them' and 'us' distinctions which an overbusy state apparatus imposes, will bring a greater sense of unity. That is why policies to reduce taxation and leave more spending decisions to individuals, and policies to encourage small enterprise and new businesses, and to create a much more diffuse and less concentrated pattern of economic power, are so vital to future social cohesion. And that, too, is why the path to a stronger common purpose lies, in a way that must seem paradoxical to the traditional socialist, not through more redistributive taxation managed by the state, but through lower taxes and greater scope for private enterprise.

However, while the restoration of the free market economy through these methods is a crucial part of our national renewal, something more is needed. My own conviction is that one of the best hopes for a prosperous democratic future now lies in the return of the ideal of personal property to the centre of the public stage, and in the widest possible spread of individual and family ownership in all its forms. It is a belief on which I shall expand in some detail later in this essay. But will the political forces in our society ever allow this more dispersed pattern of power to emerge, will the trade unions allow it, will the workers allow it?

Here I part company with a large and articulate body of opinion who take a more pessimistic view and who, like Peacock's Mr Escot, in *Headlong Hall*, adopt an insistently deteriorationist approach to our future prospects. *The Future that Doesn't Work* was the title of one book of essays in this genre,[3] but speeches and articles abound with a roughly similar sort of message – broadly that the competitive demands of organized labour on resources, plus the incurable tendencies of democratic governments to spend more, will create impossible inflationary pressures and deepening social conflict. According to this view the British disease is rampant, indeed terminal, and ensures that we have no hope whatever of 'catching up' in terms of productivity and living standards with our continental neighbours.

This fatalism has certainly infected large areas of public policy in a way that I shall seek to explore in later chapters. I reject it, not just because I would obviously like other policies to succeed and my political standpoint leads to hope that they will. I do so because I am convinced that when one peels back some of the contemporary political labels, and examines the way life is changing in Britain, it becomes apparent that despite the immensely conservative influence of British party politics, despite the outright disincentive to change built into much of public policy, and embedded in the minds of the policy-making establishment, a change of opinion, outlook and behaviour is *already* taking place, on a scale unperceived by metropolitan comment and orthodox analysis.

I am aware that this sort of optimism about social and economic trends in Britain is out of fashion. By all the conventional measures of employment, productivity, export competitiveness, manufacturing efficiency, trade union resistance to change, capacity to absorb soaring oil prices, the future looks increasingly bleak and difficult. But are these the right measures by which to judge economic vitality? Do we really understand what these aggregate concepts, which are traded around so freely, truly imply? Is the world that is visible to governments and policy-makers in Whitehall, or to general secretaries of trade unions, still a reliable guide to the world as it really works?

In what follows I shall seek to argue that other concerns and other values, much neglected in British political debate, are coming fast to the fore and that those who think about policy – and I don't mean governments only – must start adjusting to what is, in practice, going on. I start in chapter 2 with a look at this apparent disconnection between national policy and the emerging interests of another Britain, a Britain we may not immediately recognize, and yet one which now may well embrace an actual majority of the families in the country, and I suggest how the idea of personal ownership might help restore that connection.

In chapter 3 I shall take a slight excursion into a question which has always puzzled me – why the middle 'layer' in our society, the millions with what used to be called the bourgeois outlook, with a concern for property widely held on a modest scale and for the laws respecting property, should have failed so utterly to exert effective political influence, leaving the field depressingly clear for the perpetuation of class politics and of the alleged conflict between labour and capital with a vigour unmatched in most neighbouring countries.

Since this middle 'layer', in a slightly new form, far from shrinking in importance is now growing very fast, as I shall try to show, this failure is all the more extraordinary. I believe it has contributed directly to the instability and superficiality of public policy-making in Britain since the War. I must emphasize here, as I shall again later, that the 'middle' or bourgeois attitudes and influence referred to in this context represent something entirely different from the consensus approach, favoured by so many post-war politicians, which involved an attempt, assisted by Keynesian techniques, to find a middle way, a half-way house, between the supposed interests of labour and capital. It is a new 'middle' and a new way with which we are concerned.

In chapters 4 and 5 the story returns to current public policy and in particular to the way in which incomes policy and industrial policy have been, and continue to be, grotesquely distorted by wrong perceptions. I argue that those in charge of British policy have persistently misinterpreted the voice and ambitions of a tiny and politicized segment of egalitarian opinion, as being the views of *all* workers and have been, partly in consequence, blinded to vital new trends in employment patterns and in the structure of industrial and business activity.

In chapter 6 the first few arpeggios of optimism are introduced *andante*, as we look at the way in which the trade union 'monolith' may in fact be dissolving under the impact of tempestuous economic events. I argue that British trade unionism is changing in shape and attitudes, that a mood of economic realism is growing and that this now opens out the way for a much more constructive phase of economic and social policy-making, as well as a more constructive phase for British trade unionism.

Chapter 7 surveys the economic policy landscape now that the post-war orthodoxies are crumbling. I try at this point to describe and assess the character of the post-socialist and broadly capitalist society which I believe lies ahead, and the way in which it will work.

Chapter 8 sets out some of the policies which, in my view, will help this changed society into being and which will, for once, work with, rather than flatly against, the grain of changing opinion.

Chapter 9 asks how far the existing party and parliamentary systems stand in the way of change and perpetuate adversary, class-flavoured, politics, as is often alleged.

Chapter 10 tries to put the ideas and trends with which we are concerned — especially the ideas of vastly broadened personal ownership and mass capitalism — in the context of Conservative thought and the developing attitudes of the Conservative Party. It also relates them to the outside world, although this is not, of course, a book on foreign affairs.

Thus, rather oddly for a work by a Conservative politician about parties and policies, we come to traditional Conservative philosophy, to free market doctrines and their influence on the Tories and to questions of 'Left' and 'Right' in party politics, at the *end* of our short journey rather than the beginning. But this is not entirely accidental. On the whole my concern is not so much to deliver yet another Conservative message to the public but to bring to the many people who shape British public policy, some personal views about what is really happening in our country and about the ways in which the policy-makers would be wise to respond.

I share with my political colleagues the hope that there will now be a new beginning in Britain. I believe such a thing is now possible. What a Government alone can do to take the country forward is severely limited. What the British people can do, with Governments and policy-makers on their backs who cling to outdated attitudes and dangerous simplicities is not quite so limited but obviously heavily constrained. What both can do together, pulling broadly in the same direction, is very great indeed. That is the state of affairs I would dearly like to see and that is my purpose in writing what follows.

CHAPTER 2

The Thread

> Politics are the outcome rather than the cause of social
> change.
>
> G. M. Trevelyan *English Social History*

In a pamphlet 'Time to Move On', which I wrote in 1976,[1]
and also in an address I gave to the Oxford Summer School
organized by the Conservative Political Centre the same year,
I outlined my attitude to the current political debate and
urged my own political party, the Conservative Party, to
move in a new direction.

I argued not merely that with the decay of the Keynesian
system the democratic socialists had lost their way but that a
new political and social environment was opening up which
– in Britain, at any rate – could make the Conservative
Party the party of the masses if it adopted the right attitudes.

One of the keys to a more settled and less bitter future in
this country, I maintained, lay in very much wider personal
ownership and a very much wider sharing, in families and
households throughout the land, not just in the rights and
opportunities but also in the obligations which personal
possession imparts. A major element in 'democracy after
socialism' would be this central idea of the right to own, of
bringing to a very much larger section of the British people
the habits and outlook associated with ownership of some
stake in the community.

Adoption of the themes and policies of the social market economy would be a necessary but not a sufficient reason for this change of pattern. A further and less abstract dimension was required, giving people the hope that from today's fluidity this country could emerge stronger, more closely knit, more equal and freer, in the finest and most genuine senses.

A few years on, I am more than ever convinced that a major element in our weakness has been the absence of a deep, steadying layer of ownership-minded people in British society, and the absence of policies − for reasons which will need to be examined − likely to be in any sort of harmony with the emergence of such an element.

It is this which accounts in large part, or so I believe, for the quite amazing persistence of class politics and the rhetoric that goes with it at the very centre of public affairs. Everywhere one turns − to the wages scramble, the rigidity of employment patterns, the persistence of the unemployment which follows from it, the inflexible overconcentration of British industry, the preponderance of state ownership, the decline of personal responsibility, the defensive veto by the trade union leadership on new technology, the super-conservatism of British socialists − the same thread can be picked out.

Denied encouragement to own and build up long-term financial security, organized labour has concentrated overwhelmingly on short-term wage targets − with miserable results. Denied, until recently, any voice or understanding in central government, the smaller end of business has been elbowed aside, with disastrous consequences for employment and very serious implications for the future health of the economy.

Tutored to associate ownership with a narrow class, people have been ready to see it transferred on a preposterous scale to an even narrower elite inside the state apparatus. Sheltered from the 'dangerous' twin ideals of possession and obligation people have looked to government for an enormous range of

tasks, which a less divided and calmer community would be ready to organize and provide on a much more intimate and human scale.

But perhaps above all there is the fright and the insecurity which has led men and women to organize not to promote new employment but to resist it — in the totally understandable but mistaken belief that it is the 'ownership' of traditional jobs in traditional industries which alone provides the foundation of their families' security and welfare. And here lies the wicked irony; the more fiercely these views are clung to, the worse the unemployment when inevitable change comes.

The question now is whether these attitudes, so endlessly examined and deplored as manifestations of the 'British disease', are either inevitable, or in fact as deeply entrenched as they were. I do not say that one has only to look at familiar British problems through the right lens and they fade away. That would be absurd. But I do most emphatically reject the opposite — that we are doomed to an inevitable socialist order, without which the future cannot function.

I do not see it that way at all. Nor, I maintain, do the bulk of those who have been too often used as cannon-fodder in the class war. In the last five or six years British society has gone through a deep change of character as a result of its searing experiences. It could now be that Britain is riper for, and more receptive to, the application of social market economy policies, combined with policies for the democratization of capital ownership, than it has been for a generation.

In the first half of the nineteen-seventies there seemed little indeed in events or the tone of public debate to support this, scarcely a glimmer of realization in public perceptions, or in the attitudes of the leaders of organized labour, that the battles which 'had to be fought' might be the wrong ones, or that the issues might be changing. Speeches and public comment continued to depict the situation in terms of workers and wage-earners versus bosses and employers, working class versus the rest, have-nots versus haves – the classic 'Two Nations' terminology.

Today things have changed dramatically. It is not just that through super-inflation and high taxation differentials have been concertina-ed, so that the take-home pay of the manual worker or bus-driver is not markedly different from that of a sales executive, or that of a skilled worker from a professional administrator. There is another important factor to take into account. The decision of millions of women to go to work, bringing a second income into countless homes and a new and more common pattern of tastes and values to families throughout the land has pushed Britain forwards towards a one-class or classless society in a way which generations of egalitarian zeal could never do and has never done. Well over half of all married women in Britain are now seeking work of some kind. It has been estimated that fifty-seven per cent of these have part-time jobs.[2]

My argument is that this new and flattened landscape allows the emergence of a free market economy and a less centralized, less collectivized and less envious society to proceed in a way that would not previously have been possible.

Admittedly, there is one thing that has *not* changed. Britain is still the most urbanized of the larger industrial powers. Lacking a really numerous and confident peasant class, and entering the modern age with the countryside already drained of labour and the population becoming heavily urbanized, Britain was always bound to be especially prone to Marxian simplicities and to 'them and us' demonology. This meant that the myth of exploiters and exploited was certain to outlast the facts and that the myth would remain relatively easy to keep afloat for purposes of political warfare.

The politics of envy always rested on the assertion that there were two classes in Britain, the wealthy and the wage-earners. If you were a progressive Conservative or Liberal you tried to bridge the gap between the two, with hands outstretched in offered compromise. If you were socialist you confronted the wealthy and worked for the overthrow of capitalism and its replacement by the classless society and the socialist state. But either way, you accepted the underlying premise. Marxists and non-Marxists were thus united in 'diagnostic alliance'.[3]

Almost as though under a rigidly enforced conservation order this basic view of things has remained unchallenged at the centre of British politics until very recent times indeed. It is still the core of oratory at TUC and Labour Party Conferences – usually from the platform rather than from a bewildered and puzzled membership. And its reflections can be still picked up in the views of some Conservatives of the older school, who style themselves reformers in the 'One Nation' tradition of Disraeli, but who are in fact addressing themselves to a picture of society which, as I suspect Disraeli would have been the first to recognize, has long since been a parody. What he would surely have discerned instead is the enormous gulf that has opened up between the public oracles and private reality, between the world that the policy-makers believe to exist and talk about and plan for and the changing shape of everyday life as it is actually lived by millions of households.

While the policy-makers and drafters of Government White Papers talk about 'the trade unions' and 'industry' as though these embraced most people, the point has probably been reached (and if not it soon will be) where the majority of those who go to work feel that their interests are represented by neither of these entities, at least in the form they take on the national stage.

While 'manufacturing employment' continues to be the central concern of Whitehall departments, the reality is that six out of every ten people who earn their living are not in the manufacturing industry at all. They work in the service industries. The decline of the manufacturing sector in Britain, which has been depicted as evidence of growing weakness and as a trend that must somehow be reversed if economic recovery is to proceed is in fact nothing of the kind. As the economy matures, a shift into the variety of new services is inevitable, and in some respects very desirable. In 1970, manufacturing industry contributed 32.7 per cent of GDP. By 1978 it had fallen to 28.7 per cent. This does not mean that the growth of new manufacturing is unimportant. But in so far as the shift is into marketable services such as the leisure and tourist industries, finance, shipping, insurance, consultancy, broadcasting, recording, the arts, it is undoubtedly a most beneficial development for Britain, which has acquired extremely high skills and set very high standards in all these areas.

All these are 'industries' where small firms do well, where the self-employed and partnerships operate in growing numbers, where 'employment' may well be part-time, or with more than one employer, or partly on one's own account and partly for a firm or in any other one of countless patterns.

A population of which an increasing proportion spend their working hours in these occupations is bound to be changing in character and attitudes. While enormous emphasis continues to be given, in economic and industrial policy analysis, to manufacturing, and especially to large-scale manufacturing, the jobs and the lives of millions belong in an entirely different world.

Or let us take another favourite conviction in London policy-making circles – that 'out there' spreads a vast army of workers who long for more public spending, appreciate deeply the 'social wage' element in their total remuneration and hold the welfare state in reverence. What in practice can be very clearly discerned is something quite different – a widespread sense of let-down. Instead of the high hopes once placed in the 'great public services' and welfare programmes of the post-war era, there is a feeling of intense dismay at the growth of bureaucracy and centralized insensitivity which they have resulted in.

With this has come a growing scepticism about the capacity

of governments to manage sound services or to manage the economy at all by the formulae that previously seemed to simple. On all sides one can see a new open-mindedness about alternative methods of organizing our affairs, possibly on a smaller and more fragmented scale, possibly by giving more scope to the individual, possibly by greater use of price and market mechanisms, possibly by the revival of a much stronger sense of personal, as against state, responsibility in care and welfare.

'Out there' the class labels are peeling off. Enthusiasm for the 'struggle' of wages against capital is left to the professional class of politicians and trade unions, whose appeal depends on keeping the old fires burning.

But amidst all this a central question remains awkwardly unanswered. Why, if society is on the verge of shaking into a new pattern which the post-war policy vocabulary has been unable to describe – why have the pressures for change on the political and policy-making stage been so slight? Why have stereotyped views about the class conflict between wages and capital, views of the most primitive Marxist kind, which everyone thought to have been buried by the Keynesian revolution, been allowed to live on with a vigour unmatched (as we shall see in later chapters) in neighbouring countries.

I suspect that the answer has much more to do with the political feebleness of the British 'bourgeoisie' and the lack of confidence in bourgeois values in British society than with the strength of the working class. And it could well be *those* values, derided though they have been for a century in British politics and literature, which will contribute far more to the rebuilding of common ground in the British nation than any falsely labelled 'working-class' interests and demands.

In fact the derision is part of the problem. For with no sufficiently numerous group in Britain ready to stand up confidently for well-spread property ownership and the attitudes and obligations that go with it, the field has been left ridiculously clear for unrestrained class-warfare and for an entirely misleading and unnecessarily divisive presentation of people's interests.

Lacking a broad-based ownership class with any self-confidence, and the strong 'culture' and language to go with it we have lacked also the means to cope with the real changes in our society in a politically balanced way. Everything has been viewed through the 'class' lens, whether the viewer is a dedicated socialist who welcomes the struggle or a middle way apologist who hopes to temper it. Blinkered by this picture of the age we have been denied both the illuminating vision and the policies and popular pressure which are required, now more than ever, to permit the healthy development of society to go ahead.

Of course, none of this has prevented change from taking place. Below the surface of political events there is emerging what must be called a *new* 'middle' and a *new* 'way'. It is a way that people are going to take whether the party politicians come along with them or not. But the difference between a society striving to develop and change while its politicians and political ideas do not, and a society moving in some kind of harmony with its politics is very great.

I fully realize the danger of presenting things this way nowadays. People feel betrayed. What seemed like a stable platform of compromise between conserving the established order and the demands of radical socialism was in fact a moving stand, a travolator carrying the public far and fast in the wrong direction towards the collectivist destination.

But where political argument has faltered, or drifted on theoretical plains, more practical influences have been at work, checking the slide. A 'middle' society *is* emerging of its own accord, unsung, unexplained, uninspired by any very confident vision and still bruised by the manner of its birth.

It is not a child of compromise between classes, or of some political accord between socialism and capitalism, or of a grudging and precarious armistice between workers and bosses. It is the product of a maturing nation, scarred by rough experience and very poor past leadership, and now anxious to seek common ground upon which to face the future.

In the decade ahead our politics will have to adjust to our new condition and to assist, or at least not actively harm, that condition. For this we will need to call in aid all the ideals and goals of the social market economy and more besides. The skills will have to be summoned up to promote competition, disperse power, resist crude protectionism, reduce the concentration and cartelization of industry, allow a much more flexible and fragmented structure to grow in its place, organize far higher quality public services than we have today, provide carefully planned but not open-ended help for areas facing upheaval in face of market changes, the impact of North Sea Oil, and generally adapt employment, social and economic policies to a quite different pattern from that of ten years ago.

All this will have to go on while we are disentangling ourselves from detailed controls on wages and prices, and from attempts to lay down detailed targets for performance in particular industries and firms, which have no place in the social market idea. And it will have to be done while, like all other nations, we face the sharp period of adjustment imposed on us by the abrupt ending of the cheap energy era.

But if any of this is to be accomplished in our country in a way which feels just and reasonable, and which avoids a further infusion of bitterness and disillusion and humiliation, it will need to go hand in hand with a far wider spread of ownership and wealth amongst the British people and thereby a far wider measure of genuine equality of opportunity and individual and family status than anything allowed under democratic socialism.

CHAPTER 3

The Scene

The people in between looked underdone and harrassed
And out of place and mean
And horribly embarrassed.

Hilaire Belloc

It is a commonplace — but one worth uttering — that societies without a strong and influential middle layer of property-conscious people crumble into lawlessness or drift into tryanny. It is, after all, only the idea of defensible private property, whether vested in a person's wage-earning capacity or his owned assets, that distinguishes the free man from the slave, the individual from the number in the collective.

The obligations which the orderly defence of property ownership places on all members of the community, and the opportunities for a freer and more creative existence which broadly-shared property — and asset — ownership offer, these are the very essence of a settled and civilized society living in freedom under the law.

One would therefore expect to see all the political forces in Britain which oppose collectivism and support the open society rally round these ideas and carry them forward wherever the opportunity allows. In particular one would expect to see social and industrial policy arguments strongly pressed in favour of every measure which disperses economic power, whether through the reversal of industrial concentration or the enlargement of employee shareholdings in industry and other forms of worker ownership.

Yet in modern British politics this has patently not been the case. Except on the home-ownership front, where the Conservative Party in the fifties made considerable progress, under the banner of the property-owning democracy, the theme of broadened personal ownership has failed to find a place on the political stage. In glaring contrast with the majority of non-socialist and bourgeois parties in many other free countries, the political groupings in Britain have somehow found it all too difficult, a bit of a sideshow, not in the mainstream of political debate.

In this chapter I am going to suggest some of the reasons why this has come about, why this phenomenon, almost akin to chemical deficiency in the body politic, has given a sour and anaemic quality to political discussion and debate, and why this in turn has allowed bad and damaging policies to continue in Britain, of a kind calculated to suppress the vitality and creative side of the country's character and to elevate the irrational, the dogmatic and the divisive.

Despite the fearsome assault by Marx on all things 'bourgeois', the colossal contribution of the bourgeois outlook to political and social stability and progress is beyond question. By this I mean the suspicion of heroes, the dislike of adventurism and shrill doctrine in politics, the imperviousness to shallow systems of thought, the scrupulous attention to quality, the sense of local community and family. If this was a shopkeeper mentality, as Napoleon derisively suggested, it nonetheless provided the foundations for some of the noblest art and endeavour that civilization has seen, based upon massive commercial and industrial prosperity.

Above all, there was the ideal of modest and well-spread property ownership, bringing with it an equally well-spread concern that the law be upheld and efficiently administered. There was never much room within these attitudes for guilt or apology about personal wealth accumulation, or for simple theories which divide the world between struggling wage-earners and capitalists. The bourgeois mentality *understood* capital and ownership, with both the gains and the obligations they bestowed, however small the scale.

Of course the very word 'bourgeois' now seems hopelessly out of date in the British context, tarnished beyond rescue by years of denigration by class warriors, attacking from both the working class and upper class positions. But, even so, the concept deep within the bourgeois philosophy, the concept of a broadly-based structure of ownership ensuring a wide dispersal of economic power in the community, might be expected to be of enduring, even growing, importance to statemen in modern democratic capitalist societies. One would expect this to be especially the case at a time when collectivism is so discredited and defensive.

And to a considerable extent it *is* so – but, not so much curiously, in Britain. Indeed in almost every Western country except Britain a lively debate has been under way for some time not about the *principle* of broadening the structure of ownership – that aim has never really been submerged or doubted – but about the method by which, in modern conditions, the idea could be carried forward on a much larger scale.

In other words, around the free world these old 'bourgeois' preoccupations with what a man or woman or family owns, instead of being driven underground and banished from political debate and public policy, are being accorded a fresh importance in public affairs.

We may well look quizzically at the Belgians, the Germans or the French with their 'policies for the middle class' and wonder what they are all about. No-one in British politics has thought about such things for a generation. I myself remember being puzzled when, in the German Economics Ministry in Bonn in the early sixties I was handed a smart and quite fat little red volume, entitled 'Middle Class Policy' (someone had troubled to make an English version). Inside were details of numerous policies designed to meet the problems of the independent and smaller businessman, the professions and the self-employed – in fact the small 'owners'. And there, too, were details of policies for promoting personal wealth accumulation across as wide a stratum of society as possible. Since those days many more measures have been added to the list by the West German Federal Government. The Belgians go even further and have a Minister for Middle Class Interest, again directly concerned with the interests of the independent business sector and the self-employed.

All this seems worth recounting because of the staggering contrast with the British situation, where fashion and official culture have swept concern for such matters virtually out of existence.

Admittedly, as we have noted, the cause of home-ownership has made some progress and current ideas for turning the tenants of public authority council houses into owners will give this development a further substantial push. Nothing will do more in Britain, and especially in Scotland, to transform this position, and shake free the social structure from its traditional two-class mould. But while this is fully recognized by politicians, the idea of taking 'ownership' much further has somehow been submerged. The thought that there is a substantial 'middle' interest which likes to own something, which cannot be labelled either 'the workers' or 'management' and yet which should have a major and persisting influence on all aspects of public policy is considered politically eccentric, if not downright provocative.

As for the suggestion that this interest should be translated into a deliberate programme to make new capitalists and to broaden the whole network of ownership, this has been considered almost too absurd to discuss seriously and is fended off with vague and unsupported generalities: 'the workers are not ready for it', 'they want wages, not capital, which they do not understand anyway', 'the financial system could never handle asset and share ownership on a mass scale'. 'Workers would not accept the risk', 'the pension funds do the job already — it would hurt existing equity owners — there's no demand for it — the unions would never have it — we should concentrate on industrial democracy and come back to these ideas later'.

And so it goes on. What has gone wrong that there should be this extraordinary hesitancy and lack of confidence on a matter so central to the advance of a post-socialist society in Britain?

The immediate and superficial answer is simple enough. Financial and industrial leaders, far from challenging the stereotype of political and official thinking, have all too often reinforced it by taking the very shortest view. Sometimes they seem almost petrified that the diversion of future wealth and profits into broadened personal capital ownership will somehow disturb the *modus vivendi* they believe has been reached between 'capitalism' and 'the working class' and damage the already beleaguered position of existing equity owners.

This is really like arguing that home ownership should not be extended since it might damage the value of existing property. In fact, it is even sillier than that. Common sense suggests that the wider the number of people interested in capital the easier it will be politically to lift some of the penalties on capital and restore the rewards of capital to economic and efficient levels. Far from using the present atmosphere, and the present inroads of wages and salaries into the earnings of capital, as excuses for rejecting measures for wider capital ownership, the argument ought to go the opposite way. If capital is to be fairly rewarded it must be widely owned. It is as obvious as that.

Other arguments, too, are advanced for postponing a change of attitude or policy. For example, there is the contention that existing pension and insurance institutions do all that is necessary to mobilize employee savings for investment and provide a link between the worker and the process of capital formation. This enormous concentration of savings in 'the funds' is peculiar to Britain and contrasts with the wider spread of personal savings across institutions and enterprises, great and small, in neighbouring countries. [1]

One could continue almost indefinitely with the attempt to meet these suspicions and misconceptions in modern Britain about the case for wider ownership, and the resurrection, on a modern mass scale, of the 'ownership' case. But in doing so I suspect that we would only be dealing with symptoms. If we are really to understand, and, by understanding, start to respond to the extraordinary disparity of approach between Britain and neighbouring non-socialist countries, on questions of popular involvement in capital ownership, we have to return to the point where we started this chapter. We have to begin with the remarkable absence of an influential and confident voice in British politics representing the modern heirs both of the shopkeeper tradition, and of the Puritan respect for property as a responsible office, rather than a privilege, which went before it.

This essay tries to look forward from the present discontents and does not provide the best place for an historical excursion into the reasons for the urban dominance in our society, for the fading of bourgeois and peasant influence in British politics, or for its vigorous survival, in one form or another, in other free economics.

But until about twenty years ago textbooks of British economic history rightly pointed to the vast *advantage* this freedom from conservative 'peasant' politics had given to the British economy and the business community. Unencumbered by the interests of an inefficient peasant population British industry could bound ahead, with labour fed by cheap food imports. A capitalist middle class, rooted not in land but in finance and commerce, could go bustling about its business.

Admittedly, it can be argued that this capitalist 'bustle' was short-lived. Corelli Barnett maintains that it began to lose its momentum as early as the eighteen-fifties. [2] Having weakened their links with the land the British middle classes now began to turn their backs on industry as well, and attend to the task of running the Empire and manning the professions, and to the administration required to keep the new order in a settled state.

Like any thesis this one can be overstated. But something of this kind certainly went on. In fact, my own family background rests strongly in this new, middle class of professional administrators and soldiers, who turned away from commerce and managed Britain's world-wide responsibilities with skill and efficiency, until there were virtually none left to manage.

But at least this new breed of professional people and administrators, like the commercial middle class from whom they liked to distinguish themselves, had complete confidence in their world and their values. Few of them felt apologetic about middle class attitudes or numbed by doubt or guilt.

What, then, happened, to change things? Why were these people and their ideas pushed so totally out of the political scene in Britain?   ?

Roy Lewis and Angus Maude, in their study of the English middle classes,[3] select the 1880s as the decisive decade when this change of circumstances began and the sands began to shift, although of course on the surface all looked safe and solid, and was to continue to appear so for many decades to come.

But sometime about then, Lewis and Maude argue, the self-questioning, the embryo guilt complexes, began. And with the changed psychology came the weakened defence of fundamental interests. Capital was now under open attack (although on a scale that seems ridiculous today). Death duties began in 1894. The 1907 Budget taxed 'unearned' at a higher rate than earned incomes for the first time, while the People's Budget of 1909, which included a new supertax and land taxes, brought home to the increasingly demoralized 'middle' layer that redistribution of income was about to begin in earnest.

There was no stock of confidence to fall back on. The

whole British political vocabulary began to echo Marx in turning against bourgeois values and ideals. In the words of Lewis and Maude it became

. . . almost a matter of course for the middle class younger generation to be brought up on the misdeeds of the middle classes in the nineteenth century. Not only was there a century of ugliness and misery to expiate; there was the Great War, which was the result of that dreadful century. Strong and potent, amid all the day-to-day accidents of suburban life so faithfully chronicled by Punch (the essentially middle-class historian), grew the feeling that it was a reproach to be middle class at all. The word *bourgeois* was on the lips of the young; to be bourgeois was the original sin which withered joy in life. [3]

But the fatal impact for Britain fell, not on the immediate social structure but on the broad shape of political debate. In no free country were the middle classes having a particularly good time. But in many they remained a political force, ready to fight for their interests and values and to point up the dangers of new tyrannies and new unreason being advanced to replace them and their ways.

But in Britain, not so. Here the guilt seemed to stretch into the heart of politics, collectivist and non-collectivist alike. The terms 'middle-class', or 'bourgeois' remain even now a reproach in politics. The political landscape is still crowded with politicians and policy-makers ready to use them as labels of derision and contempt.

What such people thereby bless is the perpetuation of a 'class' political debate, both within and between the main political parties. The existence, or desirability, of creating a mass 'middle' ground interest is denied from the outset.

Yet the bourgeois viewpoint understood the danger of concentrated economic power just as well as Marx, whether the concentration was in the hands of capitalist or collectivist bosses. The neglect of this vital point would surely never have been allowed to persist in the British political debate as it has, and give such a polarized quality to that debate as it has, nor led to such a broad anti-property culture, if a stronger element of middle or bourgeois influence had been retained in the British political forum.

Some measure of the way things have gone in Britain can be taken by comparing the tone of the economic policy debate in the major European democracies. Over the last twenty years there has been an extraordinary reversal of roles. The axiom used to insist that the British were the pragmatists, the geniuses for compromise and common ground, the spurners of doctrine and steamroller logic, while it was Continental politics which struggled in a quagmire of passion and theory. Yet in recent years things have gone very differently. It is now the continental observers who stand amazed at the emotion and doctrine which British politicians bring to bear on economic issues and at the way the 'schoolmen' rail against each other as they advance their all-or-nothing 'answers' to the nation's problems.

In *The Open Society and its Enemies* Karl Popper has something[4] to say about this kind of political atmosphere of unreasonableness and its consequences. Popper argues that this emotional, oracular approach in human affairs is all part and parcel of the fundamentally irrationalist attitude towards the problems of social life. He contrasts its emphasis on emotions and passions with the more sober and practical approach, the 'you may be right and I may be wrong' attitude. This for him is the hallmark of rationalist political debate, although he reminds us that it is a critical, modest rationalism with which he is concerned, which sees something of the other fellow's point of view, rather than a more didactic, uncritical rationalist approach which begins by rejecting everything that cannot be proved by logical argument and ends up as a state of mind just as closed and self-contained as the theories it seeks to refute.

Popper compares his own definition of critical rationalism to the almost mystical ideology of the irrationalists, with its emphasis on deeper forces, larger-than-life heroes and its need to divide the world between believers and unbelievers, friend and foe, class friends and class enemy – a world in which pondered assessment of people's views, on their merits, is replaced by collective labels which are pinned to every utterance almost before it is made, on the basis of the 'type' who makes it. Facile typecasting becomes an easy substitute for serious critical response to the views of each individual.

The attitudes which Popper would see in place of all this, the cautious, slightly sceptical (but not totally cynical) and above all reasonable, state of mind, with its inclination towards piecemeal reform, are not all that far from the 'bourgeois' qualities I was earlier seeking to describe. It seems to me no accident at all that the Britain in which the bourgeois influence on politics and policy has been so successfully supressed is the country in which a strident, absolutist tone should have become so prominent, and the doctrines of 'Planning' and 'Freedom' set against each other with endless, ungiving zeal.

It is precisely this common sense practicality, for which England was once so famous, that has been so obviously missing from the policy debate here in recent years, with such debilitating consequences. The lack of any serious, calm and confident attitudes towards widespread ownership and the part it plays in social stability is one example. The ready acceptance of 'labour versus capital' stereotypes, postures which exclude any such thoughts, is another. The maddeningly persistent tendency for politics to continue being built round a 'them and us' picture of British society, a 'Two Nations' tableau, is yet a further aspect of the same miserable phenomenon.

All these attitudes work on and reinforce each other in contemporary Britain. Demands by trade union centralists for collectivist measures and egalitarian tax policies have been regularly met by politicians who believe that these represent the wants of the vast majority of working people and that they must be met in the interests of social stability, worker co-operation and so on.

These policies in turn have hastened the concentration of industry by preventing the emergence and profitable existence of new enterprises and would-be fresh competition. Large and impersonal units have been allowed to survive and the social and fiscal policies necessary to allow the existence of smaller units on a profitable scale ignored. The insecurity and low overall economic performance which results has led to still more union demands for defensive, anti-enterprise measures, work-sharing, employment protection, refusal to accept closures, insistence on support for non-viable undertakings, long after their place should have been taken by new and more vital firms coming up from the smaller league.

The persistence of an over-concentrated and under-challenged industrial structure then comes to be translated as a failure of management. In the sense that management is trying to operate in entirely the wrong environment this is correct. But that wrong environment is the consequence of policies pressed by trade union leaders, and supported by collectivist politicians in the first place.

The same malign influences extend into the financial arena. The high levels of income taxation demanded by the class politicians, have greatly discouraged personal investment in risk equity or directly in smaller and family firms. The savings scene has thus come to be dominated in Britain to an almost unique extent by the life and pension funds and by the building societies. That is where the wise worker puts his savings.

Some of the big funds have made valiant efforts to channel cash to the independent sector through setting aside specific sums to help small firms or through other agencies: for example, the Industrial and Commercial Finance Corporation, or the Equity Bank, or special funds set aside for small business finance by institutions such as the 'Pru'. But these efforts can only influence the edges of the pattern. They cannot possibly be a substitute for the thousand little impulses of enterprise which a lively and supple economy ought to permit, each one needing to be nourished by a little capital, a little borrowing, a little saving.

Once again, therefore, it is the small man, the would-be proprietor, owner, yeoman farmer, self-employed man, husband-and-wife partnership, that gets squeezed off the social and economic map by the 'Two Nations' calculus.

Planners and policy-makers, seeing this, cater for a static society of factories and workers, a stereotype pattern of large organizations and mass employment, in which small enterprise or self-employment are the eccentricities. The public services and the bureaucracies in turn gear themselves to a mass, standard-type, worker society in which deviation from the employee-norm immediately runs up against hurdles of regulations, extra forms, special provisions, or just non-provision. The public welfare administration also tools up for mass-production of a standard product, with MPs and councillors rising in wrath when they discover that the standard in their area is lower than, or different from elsewhere.

Thus the peculiarly coarse texture of British public policy as we know it today has been gradually woven into being – a cloth with only two tones and available only in standard widths, a pattern which addresses itself to a two-class society of workers and bosses, wage-earners and capitalists, roll-your-own fags and Rolls Royces, cafeterias and caviar, a menu deeply unsuited to the tastes, aspirations, work and leisure patterns and outlook of a very large and fast growing section of the population of the country.

Nowhere are all these deficiencies and weaknesses in the British policy-makers' way of thought better illustrated than when we turn to the arguments which rage around pay policy, the trade unions and industrial policy.

An editorial in the late seventies in the Financial Times put it like this:

The question is one of structure rather than behaviour – excessive trade union privileges conceded in the search for incomes consensus, excessive market concentration fostered in the name of industrial logic. It is these questions which must sooner or later be faced if we are to stop battering ourselves silly against the very necessary limits of financial prudence.[5]

These are indeed the questions. But where have the voices been that should have been putting them, sowing the doubts about social contracts, querying the metropolitan wisdom of industrial strategies?

In their virtual absence the political debate in Britain in the last ten years has become stranded on the Incomes Policy mudbank. Minds have snapped shut, parties have divided, 'for' and 'against', cliques have formed against each other with tribal bitterness. Issues of pay and income distribution and union power, which in neighbouring countries have been slowly hammered out, not without appalling difficulties but with a steady, practical application of commonsense views about the shape of modern, mass-capitalist society, have been here elevated into fiery uncompromises and fundamental clashes of theory.

The 'Incomes Policy' fracas is typical, in fact, of what happens to a policy-making establishment that cuts itself from an open-minded, critical appraisal of the practical problems of a changing society and indulges in emotion and doctrine. It soars above the modest, steady world of the small man and the little business, the individual and his own enterprise, the local community and the family, and latches on to impossibly general and absurdly over-worked ideas about the 'trade unions', 'industry' and other abstract aggregates.

In short, it departs from the human scale upon which most of us live and work, and from the human instincts of mutual obligation, possession, and personal and family security which concern most practical people most of the time.

In the next two chapters I turn to the ways in which this atmosphere of unbalance and unreason deluded post-war policy-makers into utterly wrong-headed attitudes about employment, about the trades unions, about taxation, about pay and about the structure of industry. In further chapters I discuss how this has diverted Britain dangerously from the path of the post-socialist, ownership-minded kind of society, towards which most of the other social market economies are busily travelling.

CHAPTER 4

The Great Exclusion

Smile at us, pay us, pass us; but do not quite forget.
For we are the people of England, that have never
spoken yet.

G. K. Chesterton

In the previous three chapters the case has been canvassed —
in a preliminary way — for finding new common ground in
British society, built among other things on the widest
possible spread of personal 'estates' in many different forms.

It has been argued that policies to help this new pattern
struggle into existence have been remarkably absent from the
British political and policy-making scene, allowing
stereotyped ideas about the class conflict between 'wages'
and 'capital' to live on with a vigour and pervasive power
unparalleled in most other mixed economies and free
societies.

One cause of this absence, it has been suggested, is the
utter failure of any property-owning, middle 'layer' in British
society to exert effective political influence, stemming from a
defeatism and crisis of confidence in the English bourgeois
classes from which British politics has still not recovered.

The results of this, it is argued, show up clearly in the
pattern of public policy, which continues in far too many
areas to start from the assumption that there is a monolithic

and unchanging working class, with identifiable and distinct working class interests, which must at all costs be appeased if there is to be any worthwhile future at all.

Finally, we went on to contend that government policies towards questions of pay and towards the trade unions have been typical of this approach, especially in the way that they misinterpret the voice and ambitions of a tiny segment of trade union officialdom as the views of *all* workers, and the way in which they tend to ignore the interests of an expanding segment of society which is acquiring a different outlook – an outlook which draws far more on the old bourgeois values than on Marxist theory or working class mythology.

The time has now come to take this point further – and not just because Incomes Policy as developed in Britain is a perfect example of the kind of thinking which comes out of policy minds closed to ideas of broadened capital ownership and focused narrowly on wages and salaries. The Incomes Policy issue is also centrally important because, together with all its related 'tail' of preconceptions and attitudes it sprawls, like some enormous and shapeless fungus, right across the path heading towards the common ground of a property-owning democracy.

Far from being a policy of consensus, the Incomes Policy as practised in Britain in the seventies, led to bitterness and division of a kind which many people assumed British society to have long since outgrown. Nor do we have to look very far to see why this should be so.

Between July 1975 and July 1978 the Labour Government published four White Papers outlining their arrangements or discussions with the General Council of the TUC and with the CBI for pay and price restraint.[1] All of these White Papers claimed that Government policy was based on the consent of the whole nation.

Now of course government policies against inflation must attract support from all parts of the community. But all parts means all parts. The TUC and the CBI are not the nation as a whole, although they are certainly an important part of it.

Within the august body of the TUC General Council there are wise and experienced trade union leaders. But it cannot claim, even on the most generous interpretation, to speak for more than half of the work-people of the country.

So how is it that an elected government felt that it could proceed on such a limited definition of 'consent'? How was it that the worries and interests of so many millions who are not members of unions affiliated to the TUC could fail to leave any mark at all on the policies or attitudes of central Government? And how is it that the voice and values of those millions have been so lost in the swirl of public debate?

Even if, for the moment, we beg the question of whether every one of the twelve million members of affiliated trade unions sees things the same way as the TUC, there are still another twelve million or more workers who get up in the morning and go to work each day. About a million are organized fairly tightly in independent unions and staff associations. Many, many more are part of the self-employed or partnership side of the economy. The bulk of these work in areas not, so far, unionized, although that may certainly be changing.

Together they make up the greater part of the private sector of the economy, they staff countless small firms and burgeoning enterprises throughout the country, they man the growing service sector, they generate new jobs, they bring capital and ideas and the organizational ability together to create new endeavours. They embrace some of the most creative and also some of the most conservative elements in the land.

The flattening of differentials, the fixed sum increment of six pounds, supported in 1975, not surprisingly, by Jack Jones, leader of the largest manual workers' union, the freezing of management salaries, the pursuit in Parliament of tax changes which bit further and deeper into business enterprise and capital accumulation than ever before, declared to be vital as part of the 'deal' with the unions — all these policies were, and were bound to be, hostile to the ethics and interests of the middle millions. Yet that is the line the Government of the day took.

How could this have come about in the nation of shopkeepers, the country of commerce and trade that grew rich through the dedication of its middle classes to the business of business? The most obvious, though not the whole answser, is that, at the time, people in all political parties, and in wide areas outside politics, were mesmerized by the events of 1974.

This is not the place for another account of the fall of the Heath Government in February 1974. But there can be no doubt that the miners' strike and the power cuts of the winter of 1973-4 greatly strengthened the conviction of the Labour Party leaders that their future lay in the closest possible liaison with TUC leadership. It also reinforced the view, throughout the political establishment, that the unions were unbeatable and that any effective policies against inflation had to rest on a 'deal' with trade union leadership.

If this meant going along with obscurantist and anti-business prejudices in the ranks of trade union activists, so be it. It was worth it, so the argument went. If it meant pursuing measures which were bound to discourage new business growth and shut off job opportunities this, too, was a price worth paying.

In all this the central calculation stood out unvarnished. There existed in the state, the argument went, a gigantic manual workers' power bloc. Its appetites were not only for higher wages and for jobs but also for more egalitarian income distribution and larger public and collective provision. If the former could not be satisfied the latter had to be. This was the position as the leaders of both the Labour Government and the TUC saw it, and a large part of public opinion agreed with their analysis, even if they did not like it.

The unasked question was whether this very traditional view of 'working class interests' still truly reflected, in the mid-seventies, the aspirations of the great majority of trade unionists and other workers, and whether these were the policies which would meet those aspirations. It was unasked because it was unformulated. And it was unformulated because the confidence to question the orthodoxy was then lacking at high political levels.

The belief that there had to be a 'deal' with the unions reflected metropolitan opinion, not public opinion. It was regarded (as it continues by some to be regarded) as progressive, in the sense that it sprang from a view of the social structure which could be shared by socialist moderates and 'middle way' Conservatives alike, and in particular by the modern Liberal Party, which sought to stand in the very middle of this 'middle'. This view was that there existed a deprived working class 'nation', and that collective redistribution and provision (high taxation and high public spending) would keep at bay not only the dangers of socialist revolution (the old progressive orthodoxy) but also the new-found power to create industrial disruption and wages anarchy (the new progressive orthodoxy). The 'comfortably off', i.e. those who owned a bit, would be saved. One 'nation' could do a deal with the other.

The significance of the calamities of 1974 is that they gave fresh life, fresh oxygen to ideas that elsewhere were dying, just as some would argue that the earlier events of 1968, when trade union influence stopped the Labour Government implementing proposals for union reform, had the same effect. After both occasions the search for a 'deal', instead of being surrendered, was pursued with fresh zeal.

Those of us in the sixties who tried to lay the foundations for the ill-fated Conservative Government of 1970, believed that this phase had passed. It seemed to us, even then, that class and envy politics were finally losing their appeal and that we might find common cause with a new generation who had no time for Marxian analysis or committed socialist trade unionism.

If we were right about the trend, we were certainly before time when it came to handling the politics of the situation. No confident, new, middle layer of society was called into being.

On the contrary, tripartite policy-making, founded on unquestioning belief in the need to placate union power, was reinforced.

A fresh word emerged to describe policy-making based on this view − or rather an old word was resurrected − corporatism. Those who used it in the most castigatory sense meant to conjure up comparisons with Mussolini's Corporate State of the thirties. This always seemed to me somewhat extreme, since what lingers in the folk memory about Mussolini's Italy, at least in British memories, is his reliance on brutal methods and 'Blackshirt' operations, rather than the finer points of Fascist economic management.

Not all forms of corporation are bad. Much of British political history has been organized on the basis of representation of corporate interests in Parliament. In fact, it is at least part of the plea of this essay that the voice and interests of many bodies and groups in our changing society should be louder than they have been.

What was wrong with the so-called corporate developments in policy-making in the early and mid-seventies was not the corporatism but its crudeness, the restriction of the right to influence policy to such a very few and such narrowly representative corporate bodies − namely, the TUC and the CBI. This placed the TUC leaders in a position which they may have enjoyed and certainly gave them great prominence. But it was hardly one which they could claim to have earned by majority democratic support. Moreover, it left the CBI in an increasingly invidious situation, apparently expected to be the voice of all business in the land when it could only be the voice of a limited part of industry. A strong revolt by the smaller business element in the CBI, plus an injection of fresh leadership less dazzled by tripartism and more attuned to the changing industrial structure, are two developments which, in more recent times, have helped lift the CBI out of the morass and have prepared it for a very different economic future to that foreseen by the orthodox analysts of the industrial and social situation of the sixties.

In this process, the late Sir John Methven played an outstanding part.

Dangerously over-simplified formulae produce dangerously over-simplified 'solutions': in the Britain of the seventies 'incomes policy', in its crudest form, has been the most glaring example. Looking back, it appears quite extraordinary that the immense complexities of pay and rewards in society, the whole centuries-old argument about income distribution, the fundamental problems of the degree and type of government regulation which can be tolerated – all these issues were swept up, in the post-war debate, into a single, impossibly simplified, hold-all idea of an incomes policy.

It was as though a great draft of immaturity was suddenly poured into the public life of a previously immensely mature nation, as though policy-making had suddenly reverted to childhood simplicities in a petulant reaction against complicated real life. Anyone with the least experience of a major pay negotiation, knows perfectly well that each claim is a political maze in itself. Each claim involves endless twists and turns of circumstance, personalities, timing, external influences, memories, ambitions, all requiring diplomacy, tact and firmness to the highest degree, if the negotiations are not to lead to explosion.

To watch the public debate in Britain through the nineteen-seventies roll all these subtleties into a simple demand for government-imposed Incomes Policy, or more incredible still, for official 'norms', was to marvel that a political establishment which was supposedly the heir to some of the wisest and most cunning government ever given to a nation should be so reduced. It was to wonder, yet again, why and when the political crafts and skills of bourgeois politics have been so excluded from public policy and why the nursery-level mythology of a nation of two classes could gain such a terrible hold.

Feeble, immature simplicity in one set of 'answers'

produced contradictory theories of equally false simplicity. Theorists of one school and another locked antlers. The Terrible Simplifier entered the stage and began to acquire bizarre authority and stature. It was as though experienced men of business, not very articulate, perhaps, but deeply imbued with an understanding of the way the world works, were being forced into the wings, put on the defensive or silenced in the face of sweeping statements which seemed incontrovertible. Keynes's superior remark about 'practical men' who were in fact the slaves of past ideas began to be much quoted again by the avant garde.[2]

Perhaps this kind of fundamentalism was bound to develop, on both left and right, as the post-war settlement broke down in failure and confusion. What could have saved the day for common sense was a strong infusion into politics and policy of precisely that kind of bourgeois practicality which Keynes, in common with many of the progressive, upper-middle class, found so boring and contempible. This was the quality that had been excluded from British politics. There was simply no room for it in the classic two-class 'capital and labour' analysis which monopolized the thinking of both middle-way conservative and socialist alike. It was the workers who had to be appeased, and the 'forward thinking' capitalists who would do the appeasing. That was to be the governing principle in any corporatist arrangements and any economic strategy concerned with the future stability of society and its currency.

Deprived of an alternative, more down-to-earth voice and influence on the British scene, politics in the seventies began to turn into an inane battleground between the upholders of this 'consensus', based as we have seen on an insensitive, inaccurate and simplified vision of British society, and fundamental counter-doctrines of equal simplicity, brought on stage from both left and right.

There are, of course, other sources to explore when one tries to explain the origins of tripartism in the particular form it has taken in Britain.

In the 1930s a major battle raged between socialist writers about the destination towards which socialism in Britain would eventually lead. Convinced Marxists like John Strachey had no difficulty in seeing what they believed to be the correct way forward — via the workers' revolutionary struggle against the capitalist classes. [3]

What shocked Strachey was the tendency towards a very different goal which he detected amongst other leading members of the British Labour Party. This goal he described as 'a corporate state, controlled, not by the fascists, but by Parliamentary socialists, and evolving, it is no doubt believed, from a controlled capitalism towards socialism'. [4]

Strachey goes on to quote with profound disapproval from the works of G. D. H. Cole [5] who, he claimed, was working with 'his friends of the British Labour Party, for a system of state-controlled capitalism insulated from foreign competition and under strong central planning direction'.

These socialist disputes of long ago have a depressingly modern ring about them. They show how readily those who feel themselves to be socialists but shrink from revolution *à la* Strachey, can slip into rigid corporatist modes of thought and action. They show how politicians who believe in something called the working class, and in the power of that class, and in the capacity of the trade union movement to mobilize that power, are driven to attitudes and measures not so very different from those espoused so vehemently by self-styled social democrats, in the seventies, in this country.

Yet another, perhaps rather drier, way of accounting for the popularity of the simple tripartite model in Britain, and also of accounting for the way in which policy-making degenerated so rapidly into such a squabble, may lie in the big change which took place at the end of the sixties in the composition of the electorate. In the 1970 General Election the numerous post-war generation voted for the first time. The October 1969 register may have included 3.5 million people, aged between twenty-three and twenty-four in June 1969, who were excluded from the October 1965 register.

Add to these, 2 million eighteen- to twenty-one-year-olds, who were first registered in 1969, and we have a total, in 1970, of up to 5.5 million new young voters, 14 per cent of the electorate.

They were clearly determined to make their voice heard and to search out new and simple truths. What post-war politicians regarded as a necessary clothing of obscurity to cover the complexities of public affairs they rejected and satirized as waffle. Everything was going to be much more straightforward and direct. People would say what they meant. It was just a question, confident young voices proclaimed, of the 'sides' getting together and working out what needed to be done to reform the British economy and British society.

If wages were the problem, then they should be planned. If prices spelt trouble, they should be controlled. If the unions were awkward they should be shown the light and brought into the established order of things to be made responsible. This was a generation and an attitude which could still drink up Keynes and drink up Galbraith. It believed the aggregates could be manipulated, the sectors planned, economics 'taken out of politics'. This was simple, straightforward and, above all, moderate. That is to say it could answer the simplicities of the extreme left and the extreme right with the 'obvious' simplicities of the centre. The only mystery was why previous generations of fuddy-duddy political leaders and statesmen had overlooked the uncomplicated nature of it all. There was no need either to 'take on' the working class or to lie down under workers' revolution. The 'middle way' could be followed by getting everyone together and halving all the differences.

It may well be that all this exaggerates the influence of a particular generation of voters. But it is certainly true that from the early sixties onwards a quite extraordinary deference began to be paid to the 'views' of youth, however half-baked, about public policy. It was as though the political establishment, having had its own authority weakened and the defence upon which it had once depended satirized and jeered out of existence, had decided that the best course was to run with the wind of the most fashionable and novel opinion, however naive, and see where it led. The stereotypes were given a further lease of life.

Westminster and Whitehall's inability to shake off the two-class perspective and to view the idea of a new 'classless class' as anything but an embarrassment and an irrelevance, meant and still means that this traditional picture of the social structure prevails. In chapter 3, mention was made of some of the bourgeois democracies, with their Ministries for the Middle Class. As was noted there, the very words sound faintly absurd in English. But the existence of such institutions reflects a realization in the central governments concerned of the modern equivalent of the 'bourgeois' and 'peasant' interest in a way unknown in the British context.

In turn this means not only that these interests and attitudes are recognized in the pursuit of broader policies but that the associated values and concerns are correctly identified as an essential part of the national interest and strengthened accordingly by government policy wherever possible.

The underlying calculation is straightforwardly political. The 'middle class' in, say, Belgium, is recognized as a mass interest and a major political force, and its consent is necessary for the furtherance of public policy. As long as the view is taken at the centre, in Britain, that no such grouping of interests is of sufficient importance in the strategic economic balance, so long will British politics retain a two-dimensional quality − to the great benefit of Marxian simplifiers, economist kings, and everyone else who stands to lose by a dispersal of collective power and authority on a much wider and more democratic base.

Finally, it is very important to understand how this frozen view of Britain's social structure carries with it a long tail of frozen ideas about the aims of public policy. For example a rooted belief in something called 'working-class interests' carries with it a very specific and dated idea of the meaning of employment. In this traditional context it means a full working week, day or night shift, spent at the place of work. The 'work' ideally should be in manufacturing something, rather than in the services sector, and in heavy manufacturing and capital goods rather than 'frivolous' consumer products, or, worse still, 'luxuries' or of course, the ultimate hedonism, candy floss manufacture.

As we shall see, from this view of employment, and from the corpus of ideas, dreams, memories and hopes which it embraces, a whole range of familiar public policy attitudes flow.

At the heart of them is a conviction that 'employment' in this special sense is an inherently good thing and should be preserved. Moreover, it should be preserved as far as possible in manufacturing industry since this is especially good. This attitude is taken even further in the current economic vocabulary and becomes the proposition that the economy *is* manufacturing industry, that employment in manufacturing is a key index of economic health and that all tendencies for this kind of work to disappear must be resisted not just for romantic social reasons but in order to prevent the productive power of the nation evaporating.

Thus the perverted aim becomes to perpetuate this kind of employment at almost all costs. Alternative work patterns, bringing with them alternative social patterns and alternative public policy needs are excluded. The fact that most people work, not in manufacturing but in services and that in every mature economy the shift is further that way, has no place in this landscape at all. The possibility that people and families may be adapting, because it suits them and suits the modern economy, to an increasing variety of work patterns simply does not enter the policy-makers' assessment.

The tendency for people to seek part-time work, arrangements by which both husband and wife work at different times to maintain the household income, the expanding habit of self-employment, the endlessly varied new services and occupations which a service-based economy breeds – none of these things fit comfortably into a world believed to be occupied by a great, working-class army, standing shoulder to shoulder in their daily toil.

The consequences are not merely that policies continue to be pursued to meet a social and work pattern which no longer exists. Even more serious, the social, economic and educational policies which a changed society requires are denied and ignored. The consent of this changed world is not sought because its existence is not recognized and its voice not heard.

At least part of the minimum wage legislation, and of the campaign of concern for the plight of those in lowly paid jobs, comes into this category. The desire to put a minimum shelf underneath the weekly wage springs from the best motives. It comes from an age when exploitation and sweat-shop practices undoubtedly obliged entire households to exist on pathetically small incomes, when the power to correct the situation through organized action was weaker and when additional income support from the state was minimal.

But today's situation is entirely different and tomorrow's will be different again. Some surveys have reinforced what common sense would anyway suggest, that large numbers of those showing up in the statistics as low-paid are in fact earning secondary or tertiary incomes in the household, and working only part-time because it is convenient both to themselves and to the type of job to arrange things this way. Ten per cent of employed men, and ten per cent of employed women are recorded by the Department of Employment Gazette as working less than thirty-six hours a week. Nearly half the 265,000 ancillary workers in the Health Service are part-timers. An NOP survey in November 1978 showed that the low-paid were most in favour of tax cuts.

Legislated increases in the amounts employers must pay for this kind of work simply legislate the job itself out of existence. The part-time jobs vanish or sink out of sight of the official arena into the world of moonlighting and the cash economy. I shall have more to say on the real-world pattern of employment, as opposed to the official and trade union picture of what people do, in chapter 7.

The era of narrow corporatism in Britain is now drawing to a chaotic close. Its end has been hastened not so much by the pressures of those millions excluded from the high counsels of tripartism as by pressures from within the ranks of trade unionism itself. The official trade union element has found, quite simply, that it cannot deliver. Trade union national representatives can talk, they can demand, they can formulate 'strategies' and propose 'contracts'. They can join in impressive weekends at Chequers or long sessions at Downing Street. But they cannot fulfil their side of the corporate bargain. Why? Because the official trade union hierarchy is only that. It is not the toughened spearhead of a unified working class but the facade which conceals the splintering of trade union power and the rejection, from within, of the whole philosophy of tripartism.

The point we thus reach is full of danger, but also full of irony. The strongest justification for the great exclusion of millions of workers and their problems from the definition of consent which inspired national economic policy was, all along, that the trade unions, with *their* unconquerable army of millions, insisted upon it. Yet, when it comes to the point, the army is not there. Enormous concessions have been yielded, much damage done to the machinery of enterprise to dissuade this great army from marching. But when the brow of the hill is reached the ordered ranks are empty and the men and women who filled them have long since gone their own ways. When the Wizard of Oz was finally challenged, after making some particularly outrageous demand, he turned out, behind all the smoke and flashing lights, to be quite a nice, well-meaning old gentleman, who was just as anxious as everyone else to escape the citadel. The bitter-comic finale of tripartite policy-making and the two-class perspective which goes with it, has been not wholly dissimilar.

CHAPTER 5

A Business People

Let us admit it fairly, as a business people should,
We have had no end of a lesson: it will do us no end of
good.

Rudyard Kipling, *The Lesson*

Britain's industrial policy, like Incomes Policy, has neglected
the new common ground. Here, perhaps even more than in
Government attitudes to pay, the policy-makers in the
seventies allowed themselves to be blinded to the major new
trends in the patterns of business and employment, which are
beginning to emerge, and which will dominate the future.

The idea of greatly broadened personal ownership in our
society has two strands, as I have tried to make clear. First
there is the concept of wider, personal, property ownership,
whether just of the home or of other assets as well, including,
in particular, shares in the productive industry of the
country.

And then there is the concept of well-diffused enterprise,
placing the productive power of the country in a very large
number of hands, in organizations both large and small, in
family businesses and small concerns of every shape and size
and in a widening pattern of self-employment.

This second point of view has remained on the margin of

industrial policy, never reaching the centre. This is because the attitudes of those who make government industrial policy derive, not from the understanding of the new forces at work in society, but from their own fixed ideas of what constitutes 'industrial logic'.

Behind this industrial logic lies a very definite view of the way advanced economies are supposed to operate.

The industrial logician starts from the conviction that the *whole* economy is visible to him, and therefore to government as well. He believes that there is a *structure* which can be identified, classified and altered.

What he cannot see does not concern him. 'Micro-firms' in their thousands, little enterprises which may be no more than a man and wife operating from home, part-time businesses, occupations involving thousand upon thousand of families and individuals, none of this can be fitted easily into the structural approach to industrial policy.

The effect of excluding from consideration the activities which take up a lesser or greater part of the working day of a significant proportion of the population is to give a two-dimensional quality to policy discussion of industry's alleged needs and problems.

By far the most articulate and readable presentation of this two dimensional variety has come from Professor J. K. Galbraith, who confidently sees the modern economy as existing in two parts.

Galbraith labels these the planning sector and the market sector. [1] The planning sector includes the giant corporations, but it also includes the whole range of major firms in the economy who are able, to a greater or lesser extent, to influence the climate in which they operate, and particularly the climate in which they set prices and control their costs. This they are alleged to do through the exercise of Galbraith's 'countervailing power' which enables them to stand clear of market forces to a lesser or greater extent and make their own rules, a process for which they are largely unaccountable.

The market sector is seen to consist of all those businesses which are subordinate to their environment and are not much good at influencing it, despite efforts to do so. This means smaller businesses of all kinds and particularly service firms, which tend to be small and scattered.

The picture presented is not a static one, not at all. On the contrary the whole burthen of this kind of analysis rests in the claim that the big are growing bigger. There is a clear resemblance here to the central Marxist tableau – ever-increasing monopoly capitalism searching with growing frenzy for markets as the rate of profit inexorably declines.

Just as with Marx, so also 'ineluctable forces' are conveniently found to be at work in the more modern versions. Economies of scale, the need to innovate – which we are told demands large-scale operations and large-scale finance – the curve of experience which enables the large organization to ride up through the learning process at once faster and more thoroughly in the handling of products – all these things, it is claimed, make the future for the poor, battered, market sector even bleaker and the certainty of rising dominance by the giants ever greater.

The analysis tips its presenters towards the predictable conclusion. There are two nations – the increasingly powerful few and the working many. It follows, does it not, that in the name of social justice, fairness and equality, the power of the few should be placed under 'public' ownership. It is this which leads Professor Galbraith to plead for his 'new socialism',[2] the new order under which the economist kings would reign 'emancipated, freed from the influence of great interests and inspired by the voice of the public purpose against the technocratic purpose'.[3] And it is this which leads British socialists to take new heart in their search for justification for the war on private enterprise. Here indeed is the case, their spokesmen explain, not just for further nationalization of the commanding heights but for the annexation of medium-sized firms as well, the 'meso-economic' power which the state must control.

Now of course there need be no surprise when the Left

argues that large firms should be taken over by the state. The surprise, or the oddity, lies rather in the acceptance of the view amongst non-socialists that the pressures for efficiency make the emergence of large units inevitable and desirable. Nowhere in the post-war world does this view seem to have gained readier acceptance than in Britain.

One might, for example, have expected non-collectivists in Britain to have championed the smaller man, both on social and economic grounds, and to have shown some anxieties about the heavy concentration of British industry. This has just not been the case − or not, at least, until the last three or four years.

One might also have expected the industrial policy-makers in Whitehall to have developed a certain scepticism about the claims for size made by British industrialists, as they pursue their mergers. But this has not been the case either. On the contrary, until very recently indeed it has been a frankly acknowledged feature of departmental industrial policy that mergers are inherently beneficial − the bigger, the better. A Green Paper published by the Labour Government in 1978[4] gave clear evidence that producer and market concentration was both greater, and increasing faster in Britain than elsewhere in Europe.

To allow these assumptions and these developments to go unchallenged plays straight into the open hands of advocates of extended social control, in the name of alleged working class interests and 'social justice'. It is as though there were some unconscious conspiracy of determination, particularly strong in Britain, to *prove* left-wing analysis correct, to vindicate Galbraith and to make the case for 'the new socialism'.

It would be just possible to understand the strength of the assumption that the trend of bigness will continue, however unwelcome it may be to anti-collectivists, if there was conclusive evidence that concentration of industry into larger units really meant greater efficiency. Then one could at least acknowledge the pressures on Whitehall industrial policy-makers to allow the process of concentration to roll on, and let others cope with the consequent political dangers.

But does such evidence exist? Experience seems to point increasingly the other way. First, at the general level, there is the obvious argument that if concentration of industry is so necessary for efficiency, and if, in Britain, the pattern has gone further and faster than in most other Western countries, how is it that Britain's productivity remains so poor?

A decade ago the confident answer was a call for still more mergers. The British Motor Corporation just was not big enough. It had to go in with Leyland to compete in world markets. Today that kind of argument looks especially absurd.

At the more specific level the case is just as questionable. Take the classical argument about economies of scale. The 1978 Government Green Paper already mentioned admitted openly that only a small part of the increase in concentration in Britain can be explained by economies of scale, and the figures to explain even that are far from decisive. The argument applies most obviously to engineering. No one can deny that mass production on the assembly line must produce economies up to a very large volume of output. That is common sense.

But the engineering and physical manufacture of a product is only one part of the production process. Economies gained in the works may be lost on the management floor, where the size of the enterprise generates a costly layer of bureaucracy and administration. Disproportionate overheads develop. Diseconomies of scale emerge. An increasingly costly management not only pushes up costs in itself but cannot cope with its huge tasks.

Even when management overheads are contained, there remain fundamental problems of coping with an establishment where so many people pass through the gates each morning that normal lines of communication collapse.

The Greeks were strongly aware of the danger of unmanageable size, and the modern army battalion is shaped by just the same considerations. Aristotle believed that a community was manageable as long as everyone knew each other by sight. Eight hundred — the old infantry battalion size — is just about the number which the mind of the commanding officer can, with a few blind spots, keep track of, in terms of remembering the face, possibly the name, even the individual problems and quirks.

Twentieth-century large scale manufacturing seemed for a time to be able to belie this ancient experience. But in recent years it has reasserted itself. Today's personnel manager would possibly advise very strongly against building plants requiring over a thousand workers. Much less would be more manageable and, in practice, more economic, whatever the engineer's calculations in favour of something larger.

So if the case for concentration ever rested on economies of scale it is now very doubtful whether it continues to do so. What about the other leg of the argument, that innovation requires large undertakings?

Of course, it cannot be claimed that size is actually against innovation. There are too many examples of brilliant innovation in major companies for that to be so. But we are here concerned with the contention that size is the *key* to technical breakthrough, new techniques and dazzling discoveries.

The closer the record is studied the harder it becomes for this view to stand up. Innovation springs from firms of all shapes and sizes. The key consideration is not scale but competition. The wider the number of firms, large and small, where bright ideas can be aired, the better for the overall development of new technology, new design and new skills. In some cases the sheer size of a research effort may actually hamper the emergence of bright new ideas. Sifting procedures, committees, bureaucratic in-fighting, can all help turn a massive research effort into a research blockage.

There is yet another reason why the argument about large units — their inevitability and desirability — should be treated with profound suspicion. Advanced economies draw more and more people into services and away from physical manufacture. There is no immunity in Britain from these developments, any more than in any other mature industrial society.

Professor Medlik of Surrey University has drawn our attention to the very remarkable figures in support of this point.[1] He estimates that in the first half of the nineteenth century a third of the occupied population in Britain was in the service sector. By the 1930s it had reached about half and today it is probably near two thirds.

In other words, in terms of occupations it is no longer correct to treat Britain as a manufacturing economy. Remedies founded on the assumption that it is one might therefore expect to be treated with some suspicion. This ought especially to be so when one considers that the service sector is now the fastest growing and most successful part of the British economy. In world markets Britain has been outstanding in selling its service 'products' with an enormous range of services in finance, shipping, insurance, advertising, consultancy, tourism, telecommunications, publishing, communications and language services generally and many more — all substantial overseas earners.

So as we move into the service economy age some of the hand-wringing over shrinking manufacturing employment ought surely to be replaced with a more positive attitude towards the enormous opportunities ahead.

An even more significant point is this. The service industries tend to be organized into smallish units. There are, of course, exceptions, but on the whole it is in the nature of a service to be offered best from a fairly small enterprise. Flexibility and imagination are the qualities called for and the human touch essential. Conditions are highly competitive, innovation rapid.

This is a future where concentration into large units is the very last thing wanted, and policies which are concerned exclusively with big manufacturing industry quite inappropriate. A complete reversal is required from the sort of priorities which characterized the so-called industrial strategy of the 1974-79 Labour Government, with its obsessional harping on manufacturing, winners to be picked (implying take-over or suppression of other 'runners') and analysis by sector in an attempt to tell the future, with near miraculous predictions about likely growth areas.

A policy which recognizes what is, in reality, happening to the shape of the economy, and the lives of the people working in it, needs an entirely different texture, and, as we shall see, a different set of starting assumptions.

So far I have been dealing critically with attitudes which have let the concentration of British industry go such a long way − on the basis of economic arguments which are largely bogus and on a path which has seemed to abandon the field to the nationalizers and statists.

But the theme has another and more positive side − the case not just *against* too much concentration but actively *in favour* of fragmentation and a plentiful spread of smaller enterprises in the modern economy.

In 1976 Graham Bannock produced a comparative study of West German and British industry which contained some eye-opening facts about the role of smaller business in the miracle economies.[6] For what Mr Bannock did was to lift the small business case from the level of pressure group politics to the centre of the debate about national economic performance.

His study pointed out that far from West Germany and Japan having proportionately fewer employed in small business (and the question of definitions obviously has to be treated with care on this point) these two 'locomotive' economies had very much larger 'tails' of this kind than Britain. Indeed, he pointed out that of all OECD countries Britain seemed to have done the most thorough job in snuffing out small-scale enterprise and encouraging industrial concentration. And Britain, of course, had one of the poorest economic records of all OECD countries.

While the ground is certainly not firm enough to link the

two phenomena conclusively, the Bannock book raises some very interesting questions on which the industrial policy wisdom of recent times has been totally silent.

Specifically, it poses the question whether small business really is the 'tail' of the modern economy at all. Might it not be that the miracle economies continue to dumbfound predictions precisely because they have remained so fragmented and *under*-concentrated, and because the small business operators have successfully mounted pressures on the policy-makers to discourage too much concentration.

In the context of British policy this is a very upsetting thought. In the first place, the implication goes flatly against the whole philosophy of the Industrial Strategy, with its emphasis on putting bits of industry hopefully together. It is also totally at variance with the big bureaucratic trade unionism which has featured so much in national policy-making. It suggests that economic dynamism springs at least as much from the small-scale, unorganized areas of economic life as from giant, capital-intensive manufacture.

From this there follows, second, a powerful argument for developing economic and industrial policies in almost exactly the reverse way, starting from a diametrically opposed standpoint, to that presently adopted. For one thing the 'small business problem' instead of being an awkward extra chapter at the end of the philippic on the great industrial future, becomes a central issue, a starting point, in the shaping of policy and attitudes. It ceases to be a separate issue, a sector, to be dealt with by Ministers and officials summoning as much patience as they have left at the end of a busy day of merger-making, and becomes instead a mainstream economic policy question.

The Bolton report on small firms [7] had it about right when it warned of the error of looking at small business as a distinct part of the economy, to be ticked off on the checklist without any understanding of the organic character of smaller scale undertakings in relation to the whole economic system.

A good example of complete insensitivity to this new pattern could be found in the thinking coming from a body such as the National Enterprise Board, which long persisted with an unreconstructed belief in the importance of 'getting firms together', reducing the numbers of firms in an industry − such as telecommunications − and using the classic and discredited arguments of previous generations of industrial planners to justify its actions.

In fact if one lays out the unfolding pattern of opinion and policy on industrial questions during the five years of the 1974-79 Labour Government it provides an excellent illustration of the wrong approach in all aspects − in the first years a heavy emphasis on large-scale industry, planning agreements, elaborate strategies for further concentration, combined with tax and social laws designed to make the climate as hostile as possible for smaller enterprise, for example through the Capital Transfer Tax as at first enacted, and through employment legislation.

There comes the awakening realization that the economy is not as the textbooks of social democracy would have us believe and that smaller enterprise has an absolutely essential and growing, not shrinking, part to play. The next phase is a frenzied attempt to modify earlier legislation to 'protect' small business from its effects.

In the Labour case this came with the appointment of Harold Lever, Chancellor of the Duchy of Lancaster, with a directive to 'do something' about smaller businesses. Modifications of earlier tax legislation began to filter through. A White Paper, Policy for the Inner Cities, was published, laying heavy new emphasis on the role of small firms. It had never been the intention, Labour Ministers protested, to damage smaller enterprise.

Yet of course a proper feel for this issue would have led to the opposite sequence. Instead of producing a full-blown new system of taxation designed to satisfy both alleged working-class ideas of fairness and the work patterns of corporate industry, and then, later, running round in circles making 'concessions' for smaller enterprise, the proper way would have been to devise a system innately favourable to small business practice and entrepreneurship, and to the maximum seeding and groth of enterprise, and then to make adjustments after that for the needs of established corporate entities.

But in the world of ideas and social attitudes, and of organized political pressures, which I have depicted in earlier chapters, the case for this alternative approach went unpursued and the arguments behind it unadvanced. The confident exponents of what might be described, only slightly misleadingly, as the 'bourgeois model' of economic expansion were just not there.

Behind this deficiency and behind the unarticulated need for changes in policy approach lie deeper considerations. First it could well be that through this lens, through the idea of smaller business as one of the keys to economic advance in the coming years, rather than as a drag upon it, the whole concept of the social market economy, with competition as its essence, could begin to acquire popular support and fit more comfortably with everyday preconceptions.

The stress on the 'social' part of the social market economy idea was always a critical part of its progenitors' thinking. Here, possibly, is one of the ways in which the hideous tensions, seemingly doomed to arise from capitalist development in a democratic world, begin to resolve themselves, given the right political expression and given policies which help rather than hinder the adjustment.

Then, second, there is a vital connecting thread between the idea of more small business activity, as a desirable end both in social *and* economic terms, and the wish to see economic power more widely dispersed and the ownership of new wealth more widely shared − in the very opposite way to that encouraged by Britain's industrial and tax policies in recent years.

The small business needs no lectures or *diktats* about industrial democracy. That is its life. The self-employed worker or the partnership needs no lessons about the advantages of personal capital building. That is what he or she is practising by the very act of working in this way.

Pressures for the establishment of a much more favourable climate for independent business in Britain than anything that has prevailed in the post-war years, and for a far greater proportion of output and employment organized in this way, go in harness with the equally worth-while aims of broader property and asset ownership and far wider participation by the workforce in the process of new capital formation.

Both trends reject the alleged efficiencies of concentrated economic power; both trends lead away from the high fashions of 'mergeritis', which have so dominated official thinking in Britain; both trends offer a far better hope of economic resilience than the brittle, bureaucratic, state-centralized system which post-war preconceptions about industry and competition have bequeathed to us.

Economic progress in a country like Britain may need the growth and natural emergence of more large firms; but that is quite different from the deliberate further concentration of economic power, with consequent pressures for more and more egalitarian redistribution of income via taxation, benefits, bogus jobs and the rest. Instead it could be that progress and efficiency actually require a far more dispersed human-scale pattern of ownership and business activity, involving personal contact and personal attitudes of a kind which the industrial revolution was supposed to have swept away.

It is economic resilience that we shall need above all. The warning about vastly increased competition from Taiwan, Hong Kong, Singapore and Korea has become a cliche. Shoppers perceived it in the High Street long before the politicians started making speeches about it. What is perhaps worth adding, though, is that in the next ten years it will all get very much tougher. Clever ideas, clever designs, clever products – these qualities and only these will prevail – especially if Britain is to take full advantage – as it could –

of the new technologies thrown up by the world energy upheaval.

The best soil for these qualities will be the smaller concern. Some vast concerns will do brilliantly, of course. But the committees, the management pyramids, the overheads, the sheer length of the communication lines, will all be stacked against them. This applies even more strongly in the service sector than in manufacturing, and it is in the service industries where the prospects not only for survival but for success for us are much the most encouraging.

British retailing techniques are proving highly exportable. They follow into markets where financial skills, consultancy services, civil engineering expertise, have long established a dominant position. The position of English, not American, as the nearest thing to a world language,has opened up further vast markets for information and learning in books, tapes, video-cassettes, for broadcasting and transmission. All this tends to be the arena of the smaller enterprise, the bright, small group of people who can translate flair and imaginative thinking very rapidly into the product or the service, and on top of that can then organize and deliver the service in a reliable form.

Moreover, it could be argued that while independent enterprise is in itself an expression of broadened and dispersed capital ownership, it also provides perhaps the most favourable ambience for sharing the growth of the equity with the employees. One cannot prove, nor would I wish to, that larger schemes in large firms are bound to be less effective. But the smaller outfit, or the business which has grown fast from small beginnings with the same personnel, many of them committing not just their working hours but their whole lives and emotions to the firm's performance, – this type of firm is obviously exceptionally well-placed to develop schemes, spreading the ownership of the equity, and of course many have done so, despite a hostile tax climate.

It is now slowly – and by some, reluctantly – beginning to be understood in Britain that the expansion and vitality of the smaller enterprise part of the economy is a central theme, not a marginal social problem or a piece of economic nostalgia. It is slowly beginning to be seen that if policies are to be built upon consent, those policies cannot and should not exclude the views and interests of this large and growing element of society.

There has been, in the precise sense, a revolution, a turning over of attitudes and standards, hastened on by the ever more visible deficiencies of the present pattern. In the next chapter I shall trace the course of this revolution, and of the crisis of socialism in Britain which has accompanied it, and how the new currents now running in British society bring both dangers and hopes for the future.

CHAPTER 6

The Turning Point

> But the vicious circle has never ceased to revolve. Wage
> demands have led to inflation. Inflation has led to a
> demand either for a price freeze, or a wage freeze or
> both. The demand has been met. The result has proved
> intolerable and unsustainable. The freeze has melted.
> The accumulated dissatisfaction has resulted in an ugly
> rush to raise prices and wages. The inflation has begun
> again, and the circle is complete.
>
> Lord Hailsham, *The Dilemma of Democracy*

Has there really been a turning point in Britain, the
beginnings of a change in society's understanding of what is
wrong and how, step by step, it might slowly be altered?
Many people who are by no means normally of a pessimistic
turn of mind would say that the prospects are as bad as ever,
as we move into the new decade and that nothing
fundamental has changed at all. Some would claim that we
are travelling along exactly the road charted by Aldous
Huxley[1] and George Orwell[2], to the point of total
manipulation and suppression of individualism. Those with
less apocalyptic tastes might argue that we are all set for a
pattern of anaemic corporatism, a kind of uneasy baronial
settlement between the great corporate interests, in which the
victim will continue to be the creative and imaginative spark
which once gave British society the vigour to compete and
succeed.

Governments may come and go, this thesis continues, but none of them will make much difference, or halt, more than momentarily, the inexorable drift downwards to a greyer, shoddier world. Having refused again and again, as a nation, to face economic realities or to fight for our economic liberties, we, the British, will sink to a lower level of existence, possibly more anarchic, possibly much more ordered, or with one state succeeding the other. But either way Britain will slide further and further behind the other free economies in performance and influence, becoming not so much a pleasant back-water as a grubby backyard of incompetence, narrowness of out-look and impoverishment.

My own view is that if Britain was previously on this kind of course, it no longer is. A change *has* taken place, although only very recently, at a very fundamental level, in the mood and outlook of the British. One does not need to give a precise date, but I am sure that the turning point was sometime around the financial crisis period of 1976, culminating in the massive intervention of the International Monetary Fund in British policy, when the mood really began to swing into a new direction.

The process I want to try to identify is exceptionally difficult to describe because so many of the conventional indicators – on which misleading assessments and bad policies have been built in the past – continue to point firmly the wrong way. Sizeable parts of British industry, like motor manufacturers or shipbuilders, face ever increasing problems. Whole areas, like Merseyside, appear to be destined to indefinite contraction and decay. Taxes remain high, in Britain even after recent cuts in top income tax rates, and class politics are still very much in evidence. Above all, the trade union movement still appears, on the surface, to be as firmly as ever in a position to veto the changed industrial, fiscal and social policies which would both reflect and further encourage an altered national mood.

Of course, if we were to resign ourselves to the prospect of monolithic and obstructive trade union power this book would stop here. The next stage in society's development would be all too easy to predict.

The trade unions would continue to prevent the introduction of social market policies which might halt and reverse the centralization and socialization of Britain. The independent sector would continue to shrink, the economy to ossify, and the share of profits in the national income to contract. This in turn would make it less and less attractive to investment, thus giving a further downward twist to economic performance.

Labour politicians would then move swiftly to the next stage of corporate collectivism – the control of investment funds in the name of 'organized labour', 'the British people', 'social purposes' or any other collective identity or phrase thought to be persuasive. Whether this was recognized as socialism or corporatism, it would in practice keep us firmly in the mould of the two-class, divided society, with the new ruling group, the bureaucratic owning class, having almost complete control of the capital instruments of production and the rest living on allocations decided from above in accordance with what were deemed to be their needs.

In his book *Enemies of Society* Paul Johnson describes the decay of two-class Rome:

By the time of Constantine's death, the Roman Empire had become a totalitarian state in both an economic and a political sense . . . . The middle element in society was wholly eliminated in law, and mankind was divided into two classes, the *honestiores* or upper classes (landowners, high officials and clergy), and the *humiliores* – everyone else. Each category had separate functions, rights and punishments. The corporate state was complete.[3]

But ours is *not* complete. We are not yet the *humiliores*. This essay would be a pointless exercise if I thought that ours, too, was a Roman future, or if I was not convinced that forces are now at work which are fast dissolving the union monolith and its surrounding mythology. In practice I believe those forces to have gathered enormous, almost revolutionary, strength in recent years in Britain and to be now confronting Britain's policy-makers with a totally new situation – one both of great danger and considerable opportunity. Far from the British trade union movement reaching the end of the seventies united and politically dominant, it limps into the new decade more fragmented, weaker and discredited than at any time in its history.

The dangers in this become increasingly plain at each spasm of industrial unrest in Britain – the collapse of centralized union authority and the rise of scattered and anarchic local power, reluctant even to wage organized class warfare and ready only to pursue its own narrow ends, regardless of all wider interests.

But while this rejection of union leadership is partly anarchic, it is partly, too, the very opposite. For every shop-floor militant who disssociates himself from his national union leadership for the failure to pursue anti-capitalist policies with sufficient zeal, there are dozens who turn against the leadership for quite a different reason, which has nothing to do with left wing political agitation – namely, the undisguised failure of unions to deliver greater national prosperity or higher living standards for all workers and to recognize aspirations for a better status for working people than working-class ideals traditionally offered.

For a while, at the end of the seventies it looked as though these two attitudes were intertwined, combining to give trade unionism its present appearance of general disintegration. Both provided golden opportunities for militant unionists to make the running. But in fact the two underlying elements are certainly different. If the political leaders and policy-makers of our country fail to distinguish between them, then it is possible, I suppose, that the anarchic element could predominate, with a totally disastrous outcome for British society.

But, given the right appreciation of the motives and outlook of the vast majority of trade unionists and given the right policies following from that appreciation, I do not see that victory for anarchy is at all inevitable. On the contrary, the melting of the old monolithic union power could give precisely the opportunity the country needs to move forward, away from division, and onto the common ground of mass ownership and unity of values once again.

For this appreciation to be the right one, and for the policies which flow from it to lead in the right direction, it is vital that the root causes of the pressures now working on the trade unions should be correctly understood.

These pressures come from two directions. First, there is the collapse of the social democratic dream, the failure of the belief that non-revolutionary socialist redistribution and planning could deliver a high standard of living for all. Second, there is the changing character and structure of the whole trade union movement itself, putting an increasing gulf between the left-wing mythology of the trade unions and the actuality.

British workers are now amongst the low earners of the West. The decline has admittedly been relative, rather than absolute, over the post-war period and for the escapist there always remains the avenue of argument that the statistics do not tell the whole story, that in all sorts of immeasurable ways the quality of life is better in Britain than in Germany, France, the United States or Japan (otherwise why do so many of them want to come and live here, and that, anyway, this is the way the British like it, so why upset things?).

But when this speech has been delivered the intrusive reality remains. In a decade Britain has fallen in the living standards league from the bunch at the top (France, Germany, Holland, Belgium) to the bunch at the bottom (Spain, Portugal). Between 1963 and 1976 average net take-home pay rose by less than *one per cent* a year in real terms. Between 1973 and 1978 it dropped back. The quality of life, in the most obvious sense, has deteriorated. That is to say that fewer families feel they ever have a bit of spare cash to spend or put aside. Household budgeting gets tighter, family arguments more tense, under economic strain. Outside the front door the surroundings are often getting scruffier, not cleaner, and life outdoors certainly more dangerous and violent after dark. Hopes of lifting oneself and one's family out of the rut, out of the weekly wage scramble and out of tenant life on a not-very-pleasant council estate, have become, over the years, more, not less, remote. Public services have been getting worse, not better, queues at the hospital longer, schooling patchier, yet deductions and stoppages on the wage or salary slip – the 'social wage' to pay for it all – had by the beginning of 1979 grown greater than ever before.

Against this sort of background even the most fanatical devotees of the policies and demands of the trade union leadership in recent years now wonder whether they really have been on the right track. In fact the signs are that a great many trade unionist rank and file are doing more than wondering and are beginning to be shocked into questioning very seriously whether the standard catalogue of demands for a bigger social wage, more income equality and more nationalization are really what they want. That is certainly what they have had. Even now I am not sure that all political opinion fully understands just what a remarkable narrowing in the range of incomes has taken place in Britain. Nor do the official statistics tell the full tale.

A good example of the difficulty experienced by minds clogged by stereotypes in adjusting to the facts, emerged during the 1976 Commons debate on the Finance Bill of that year. At the time, a crusade was still in full flower against the fringe benefits of the over £5,000 a year class – a category which was presumed to consist of directors and other 'non-useful' people, and certainly not to contain anyone who could be described as an ordinary decent worker. The atmosphere was similar to that prevailing when the Capital Transfer Tax legislation of the year before had been writing the death sentence of many small businesses and vastly reducing the incentive to grow new ones. Here, too, the old believer could proceed into the attack with confidence, since surely this was part of the ruling class interest and nothing to do with the interests of the workers.

In the case of the £5,000 a year figure, Labour back-benchers showed astonishment and disbelief when it was explained that roughly a quarter of the nation's workforce already grossed more than £4,000 a year, which, with the odd perk or two, would bring them right into the despised grouping.

All these figures have been long overtaken. By the Autumn of 1978 over three million 'workers' were earning over £100 a week, or £5,000 a year, according to the official Earnings Survey. Average earnings were £88 a week. By the Autumn of 1979 the figure was £100 a week and by 1980 over £120. 'Workers' here goes in inverted commas because the use of the word in this context seems to imply that those not included in the survey are not, by some strange stereotyping, real 'workers'. Thus the millions who do not fit neatly into a particular employment category, or who are self-employed, or who may draw their income from several jobs, or who may draw a second income from savings do not show up in surveys of this kind.

Nor can a picture of this nature reflect the full extent of the change in households, in about half of which the wife now goes out to work. Nor, of course, can it tell us anything about the invisible economy of undeclared earnings.

None of this would be so significant, except as evidence of the ravages of currency depreciation, if the same proportionate increases had been registered at professional, management and entrepreneurial levels. But this is very far from being the case. A graduate engineer with several years' technical experience came out of the nineteen-seventies earning less than the average manual wage. Earnings for semi-skilled work went as high as £6,000 and £7,000, well into the earnings range of the sales manager and the middle-rank executive. Skilled worker earnings of £200 and £220 a week were reported — again figures now dwarfed by more recent 1980 reports of earnings in some skills.

Compare all this with the salary landscape above, say £10,000, where successive pay policies imposed a near freeze and one can begin to see the extent of the change in relative incomes, even before tax. Add to this the sky-high marginal rates of income tax which operated in Britain through the seventies and it can be understood how, over an enormous range of workers, whether blue collar or white collar, and whatever class the old stereotype might have put them in, net differentials have been compressed almost to vanishing point. As far as available weekly spending money is concerned, the situation is not all that different whether one is in management or the manual grades. In some public services it is a bitter reality that the overtime grades take home substantially more than the management, whose traditions do not recognize the idea of overtime, since they are always 'on'.

And what is emerging out of this immense change? Certainly not a contented, egalitarian, society of socialist workers. Far from it. Much greater income equality may have come, but not the mass contentment that was supposed to go with it. This is a nervous new world, with its own new hopes, fears and problems. On the council estate and the owner-occupied estate views are converging. The concern in both is increasingly with the staggering tax stoppages and national insurance deductions on the weekly or monthly payslip, the lack of incentive to stay in work, or go to work at all and the feebleness of the authorities in righting the balance.

This is certainly not the language of the old, working-class solidarity. There is no talk about the glaring inequalities of income or the burning need for more public ownership to be found on these doorsteps. What we have here is the angry and bewildered voice of those for whom the old class labels and union battle-cries have not the slightest relevance, even if they had any before.

It is possible, I suppose, that the old middle-and working-class distinctions could reappear as before. But my own conviction is that in the compression and high temperatures of inflation attitudes have changed for good. Of course the whole experience has been harrowing for the middle income groups who have seen their living standards severely reduced. But the new situation could well present an immense opportunity to break out of the disaster spiral. If we are looking for the first signs of a turning point in public perceptions, a final rejection of the class fallacy, a new readiness to embrace the values of a more stable and solid kind of society than anything reflected in politics in post-war years, then I think we are now looking in the right place.

As an increasing slice of Britain's workforce, from all occupations and backgrounds, begins to see the world through the eyes of their new and shared circumstances, a shift in this direction becomes not only desirable from the point of view of a more settled future, but also, at long last, possible. Causes for which the old, working-class culture and its vociferous champions had no time at all – such as the individual ownership of homes and wealth-creating assets – could acquire fast-growing appeal. Governments which continued to commit themselves and the nation to vast general goals such as faster economic growth or 'full employment', or massive income redistribution, in the belief that these things were what the workers wanted, could find themselves carrying less and less conviction with a public increasingly attracted to entirely different ends.

In short, the reintroduction of a proper ladder of incentives and rewards could actually become easier with the rise of popular preoccupations with grades and career structures and status, and not more difficult, as might be feared by those who wrongly diagnose the climate of frustration and unrest as an occasion for yet more concessions to alleged working-class demands, and yet more egalitarianism.

The second set of pressures mentioned earlier related to the changing character of the trade union movement. Britain's trade unions are highly competitive. This, of course, goes somewhat against the romantic idea of a vast movement united in solidarity against the capitalist classes. This latter idea belongs not to the world of tribal inter-union warfare so familiar in Britain today but to the mythology of the trade union movement which is something entirely different.

In order to see how wide the gap has now become between myth and reality, it is perhaps easiest to begin with the three popular beliefs about trade unionism in Britain. They can be summarized as follows: that trade union leaders, and the TUC General Council in particular, speak for all the people of this country who work; that what trade unionists want is more socialism, which is best achieved through unanimous support for the Labour Party; and that the trade unions reject the market economy as being bad for their members' interests, offering instead brotherhood and co-operation in a form which protects workers and raises their living standards above the level at which, in a free market situation, they would otherwise be.

How true are these popular assertions? Opinion surveys may not be all that reliable, but they do suggest that a large number of trade unionists see things very differently and are worried by the conflict between fact and official fiction.

About 26 million people in Britain go to work or seek work. About 12 million of these belong to 'proper' trade unions – i.e. those affiliated to the TUC. Admittedly, the word 'proper' is offensive to many hundreds of thousands of other workers, who are organized in staff associations, and groups run with scrupulous attention to carefully-laid-down rules. Some of these have come under great pressure from affiliated trade unions to stand aside and others have felt it necessary to seek affiliation, bringing a changing flavour to the trade union movement as a whole. But let us start with the overall statistics of the TUC and with the means by which power and influence at the top has been hitherto sustained.

Of the 12 million members about 6.2 million are members of the Labour Party by virtue of their decision not to 'contract out', in other words their decision not to decide independently but to allow the union authorities automatically to collect a sum from their wages, over and above basic union dues, which forms a political levy and is invariably paid to the Labour Party.

These 6.2 million are represented inside the Labour Party by a limited number of trade union leaders who wield their votes en bloc in support of, or against certain policies. Thus, on paper, a solid working class political interest does indeed exist and continues to be deployed decisively in favour of collectivist policies. In fact it totally dominates the Labour Party, since beyond these millions of block members there are only some 650,000 individual members of the Party, and even this official figure is probably well on the high side. The official figure for 1978 was 676,000. An article in *Labour Weekly* on 28 September 1979 said this figure was 'utter rubbish', adding that *Labour Weekly's* own guesstimate puts it . . . at 284,000! In effect, the union block vote *is* the Labour Party.

But things are not as they seem. First, it appears that a large proportion of those who pay the political levy, and whose votes are thus used in support of certain political aims, are unaware that they pay, let alone that they are voting for socialist programmes. This proportion may be as high as thirty per cent!

Second, the people who use their votes and claim to represent them in doing so, have fairly slim grounds on which to rest these claims. In 1979 no one on the TUC General Council had been elected by more than 25 per cent of union members' votes, some by much less. Some union leaders are not elected at all, they are appointed.

It is also true that the way in which votes are collected in trade unions is sometimes very peculiar, and, alas, in one or two cases has been found to be fraudulent.

All in all, it would be surprising if anything more than a fraction of the 6.2 million agreed with the views so forcibly expressed on their behalf as the 'demands' of the workers. In practice, every survey of opinion suggests that support for, say, nationalization of banks and insurance companies is minimal. This, however, did not stop the policy being included in Labour's 1976 programme by almost 6 million votes to 122,000.

Even if we really were hearing the true voice of the 6.2 million when their leaders speak, there are the other millions inside the movement to consider. The big percentages contracting out, i.e. taking the often quite brave decision to tell the shop steward that they do not want to pay the political levy – are to be found in the white collar unions. For example, about sixty per cent of ASTMS members contract out, although this does not prevent the leadership of the union taking a strong collectivist and 'class war' position on most issues.

This in turn is a reflection of a very important change in the trade union movement. It is no longer dominated by a romantic, unquestioning, class outlook. A new and very large, white collar element has emerged. This new block may retain some of the characteristics of traditional trade unionism, including its urge for job preservation, its readiness to bargain for narrow interests ruthlessly (perhaps even more ruthlessly than the older manual unions) and its fondness for high public spending (mainly because we are talking about unions which organize very large numbers in the public sector).

But its members are certainly not working class in the traditional sense and they are not so interested in socialism and the Labour Party. While the old guard deliver weighty harangues about the virtues of Labour governments, and the need for undying support for Labour, these new elements fidget and look bored. They will support not the government which promises socialism, but the government most likely to give them what they are after, and that is beginning to be a very different thing.

For many trade unionists the difference becomes starkest when they study official trade union attitudes to industry. For while the policy of some of the national leadership continues to be couched in the language of large-scale manufacturing and planning, the reality is that increasing numbers of rank-and-file members do not work in this kind of environment at all. They work in public and private services, in smaller enterprise and in the independent sector. For them the ponderous, almost Wagnerian tones of socialist trade union leaders, with their talk of the millions marching shoulder to shoulder towards the socialization of industry, the destruction of profit and the triumph of collectivism in a better world, have no appeal whatsoever.

Nor does it make such sense to this growing proportion of Britain's trade unionists when they hear about the evils of the market economy and the virtues of large-scale industrial planning and the greater brotherhood and prosperity alleged to prevail where workers gather *en masse* and union political power is strongest.

On the contrary, experience tells them that the smaller, and medium-sized enterprises are the best ones to be in. Wages and conditions are often better, participation in deciding the way the firm goes often far greater, longer-term rewards, both in job satisfaction and in opportunities for building up personal capital and giving the family a better life, often much larger.

So far I have been dealing with workers in trade unions. But as I have pointed out, over half Britain's workforce are outside trade unions, some of them organized, most not, a growing number partly or wholly self-employed. Chapter 4 traced the way in which this 'majority' had been persistently ignored by politicians, until recently, in the making of economic policy, although since 1976 there have been moves in the Labour Government, of almost comical panic, to reverse this. So, if we add together the millions of paid up trade unionists who work in smaller enterprises and in services, with the 12 million workers who are not trade unionists at all, we get for a moment, as through clouds parting, a startling glimpse of a totally different workers' world from that presented to the politicians and the public by trade union political activists and by committed socialists.

But it is only a glimpse that we are allowed, because the official climate of opinion hardly dares admit such a prospect. The whole of public policy has been built round quite different views on the question of who 'the workers' really are, where they work and who speaks for them. The needs of this other world we have glimpsed have not been discussed or considered, although it clearly embraces *the vast majority* of those who earn a living in the British economy.

The near revolution in British society that has taken place in the seventies has brought more of these millions on to common ground, and made them more aware of their common needs than anyone a decade ago might have dreamed. Their needs are not the needs of 'the trade unions' as interpreted by some trade union officials but of all those at work who want to negotiate and act responsibly in the interest of higher living standards, better status, a stronger say in the community and a more interesting and satisfying occupational pattern.

In policy-making terms, therefore, this new 'class' of almost everybody has two major interests. The first is to see that public policy in all areas does the maximum to permit responsible effort, responsible earning and responsible owning. The second is to see that policies which prevent those at work and in trade unions from acting responsibly and reasonably, which place the power to suppress any such impulses firmly in the hands of those who put their very political idea of the trade union 'interest' before the real interests of the workers, should be changed.

This, of course, raises the sensitive issue of the legal powers of trade unionists. This was the issue of 1969 and of 1974, how to let responsible unionism out of the trap into which it had been led, less through its own inherent faults than through the imposition of socialist policies and attitudes on the whole employment pattern.

The two broad strands, more opportunities and incentives for the responsible, less power available for abuse by the irresponsible, go together. They are all of a piece. Trade unionists may become convinced in increasing numbers that collectivism is not what they want and has done them no good, but they are not going to be moved to mount pressure for change if the alternative seems to be a return to traditional capitalism, a switch from undemocratic and divided socialist society back to equally undemocratic and divided capitalist society. There is no gain along that path. As well go along with the devil you know and the socialist policies which have done no good but which are surely better than what went before.

Nor can there be any point in pressing for change if the immunities and privileges which surround trade union leaders and their actions make them impervious to change anyway.

Yet this is where those who are supposed to have led reformist thinking have all too often started to mumble and make for the door. It all seems too difficult. After all, the trade unions put a stop to any change in 1969 and it is generally felt that a repetition of the 1971 Industrial Relations Act would be a disaster, would drive millions of would-be responsible trade unionists back into the arms of the militants and generally put a stop to the very changes which need to be encouraged and of which there are so many incipient signs.

Yet I do not myself see any way round the issue. Either we permit the growth in Britain of a modern trade union movement, operating in a spirit not very different from organized labour in neighbouring continental countries, with broadly the same position at law, the same protections, but no more and the same balance of power when it comes to industrial action, or our progress remains paralysed by a totally unrepresentative minority, tied to the Labour Party.

The key issue is not really the extent of legislation, or the degree of reliance on codes of practice, or when and how such measures should be brought forward in Parliament.

The real problem is how to make any new patterns of behaviour accepted and welcomed. And here it seems to me that the idea of broadened personal ownership has a major, indeed an absolutely central, role to play. For we must be clear about the strength needed by any countervailing force if the road-block of trade union power-for-collectivism is to be shifted in Britain.

If socialist ownership and socialist redistribution are going to be finally recognized as a fraud, then the alternative must offer something not merely better than socialist practice but as good as socialist promise – in other words, secure incomes for millions of households, opportunities for a full life for all the family, complete equality before the law, and a well-dispersed pattern of economic power, on lines totally different from the practice of socialism, certainly, but also different from the popular memory of capitalism.

This, to my mind, is why general statements, however finely couched, about the virtues of the free market, the obvious advantages of the capitalist system and the importance of the individual in the scheme of things, are just not enough. They are not enough to reassure bewildered millions of workers that change is worth fighting for or sticking one's neck out for. And above all, they are not enough to convince the vast majority that the time has come to support, demand, insist on, a change of philosophy at the head of the trade unions and the Labour Party, if necessary by changing the laws which give too much power to union officialdom to impose its own attitudes and to exclude those it does not like.

If, however, it can be shown that power to the state and the bureaucrat really can be replaced by power, status and prosperity for the worker, if it can be shown that patterns are within reach which would open up the freedom of property ownership to millions, giving escape from the wage-dominated scramble and opportunity for independence, on a scale which no system has so far delivered, then it seems to me that the chances of letting responsibility flourish, of working with the real grain of mass opinion and of escaping the extraordinarily durable tyranny of stereotype class politics are vastly enhanced.

This is why the next chapter leads on to the ways in which this route could now be followed. I want to try and show how schemes for broadening personal ownership and creating capital estates on a very wide scale — schemes already operating in the bourgeois democratic economies around us — could be introduced and made to work.

But before we reach this point a further excursion into political economy is required. For we need first to see how the economic theories, as well as the political preconceptions, that have dominated British policy-making for decades, are crumbling away and making a capital-owning democracy not only a possibility, but a necessity.

CHAPTER 7

The Unofficial Future

> I must see the things; I must see the men.
>
> Edmund Burke

The citadels of post-war economic orthodoxy have fallen. Few would now dispute that. The Keynesian interlude is over. Gone is the confident belief that the expansion of demand by deficit spending, combined with vigorous income redistribution can sustain economic growth without inflation or create a climate of justice and fairness. Gone is the confident hope that governments can deliver full employment.

But what is to come in their place? The revived concern in Britain with monetary influences on price movements and on the business climate is clearly desirable and welcome. But equally clearly it is not enough. As Britain's poor industrial performance continues to show, it is possible for a nation to maintain a broadly sound framework of financial policy and yet to batter itself amost insensible within that framework.

Keynes saw and feared the instability of the capitalist system of the twenties because it could not ensure adequate employment when in equilibrium. Post-Keynesian monetarists feared the inflation and instability arising from Keynesian remedies, particularly when crudely applied by those who only half understood what Keynes was saying. The primacy of monetary restraint is now reasserted.

But neither the Keynesians nor the neo-monetarists in Britain, in their search for stability, have had much to offer in face of the enormous tensions which in a modern deference-free society all the conflicting claims, including those of the state, generate. Keynes had little to say about the propensity of politicians to meet asserted needs on all sides without regard to the limitations of resources. While for their part the monetarists cannot guarantee that the controls on the supply of money will be free of intolerable political and group pressures. As Sir Keith Joseph has pointed out, it is possible to combine apparent monetary rectitude with a level of state spending so large in relation to total resources that the enterprise sector of the economy is progressively undermined and the social tensions caused by an excessive government 'take' mount up dangerously.[1] This was the new and highly volatile 'socialist monetarism' which emerged in Britain after 1976.

So the search for stability and for reconciliation between labour and capital continues. In 1958 a book was published in America called *The Capitalist Manifesto* written by Louis Kelso, a San Francisco lawyer.[2] The central message of *The Capitalist Manifesto* was powerful and simple. It was that capitalism would only win lasting universal support if it was universally applied, if private ownership came to be commonly regarded as the promoter of fairness and equality rather than as the enemy of these things.

Kelso criticized Keynes for not giving attention to this aspect and for placing his hopes in 'full employment' policies as the best means of securing some kind of capitalist future. He warned his readers that despite 'the prevailing sense of well-being' they were marching with these policies into an inflationary ambush. He also went on to argue that Marx was right to be preoccupied with the progressive concentration in the ownership of capital, although wrong not to see that the concentration of economic power in the hands of the state bureaucracy would lead to even greater evils, and wrong to ignore the third possibility, ownership of the instruments of production directly and individually by the masses.

These were brave things to say in the high noon of post-war prosperity and the Keynesian consensus. It is no surprise that while they had some popular impact they made little impression on the confident economic thinking of the period. Nor were they entirely fair to Keynes, who in *How to Pay for the War*[3] showed that he was aware of the inflationary pressures on monetary policy which would flow from constantly escalating wage rates and suggested that this might be to some extent eased by giving workers 'a share in the claims on the future which would belong otherwise to the entrepreneurs'.[4]

But the idea of broadened capital ownership as the stabilizing factor in a world which would just not be able to produce enough viable wage-earning jobs, in the old sense, sets such ideas apart from the run-of-the-mill attacks on Keynes and helps to point a way out of the labyrinth.

The Kelso 'doctrine', with its firm commitment to the principle of private property on a mass scale, has left virtually no mark on British policy thinking. Instead, British thinkers, faced with immense union pressures for deficit spending and with the rise of increasingly aggressive collective bargaining, have been driven to the two despairing and polar conclusions. Either the system must be brought under increasingly centralized control, with as much cajoling of the union politicians on the way as can be managed, or, at the other extreme, the politicians must turn on the monetary squeeze, cover their ears and wait for the bang, after which the surviving parts of the economy will proceed sadder, wiser and more responsible. Either we go on to more central planning and authoritarianism past Keynes, so to speak, or back to the crudest precepts of free-market capitalism.

The theme of earlier chapters of this book has been that there *are* paths out of this dilemma, that an increasing number of people in British society are anxious to follow those paths but that at the political and policy level, the impulse to react has been missing.

A major difficulty is that the word 'capitalism' freezes thought. It is seen as part of the past, not capable of development, except towards contradiction and destruction.

We need to stand back for a moment and look at the capitalist system not only as it has been and has become, but as it could be.

The *primitive capitalist model* is distinguished by heavy private concentrations of capital (which were the object of Marx's attack) and subsistence earnings for the non-owning wage-slave masses. Under the *state capitalist model* all capital is publicly owned and labour remunerated by distribution according to needs, meaning bureaucratic judgment on the basis of various ruling caste views about what people should have.

Under *mixed modern capitalism* ownership is still relatively concentrated in state and private hands and distribution is determined partly through welfare policies and job-support policies and partly through trade union pressures. The losers in this pattern are the capital owners whose returns are eroded by political and union pressures – a development which the state and very big institutional owners can just about stand but which obviously steadily undermines the attractions of holding capital on a smaller scale. One only has to compare the situation of the skilled wage earner with that of the small-time landlord or small investor to see how that is working out in Britain.

This, in essence, is the *'anti*-bourgeois' model, in which the whole weight of public policy is gradually shifted against the rewards of capital and property ownership and in favour of alleged demands for satisfaction solely in terms of wages and salaries. The shift continues as long as political pressures are behind it and as long as countervailing influences on policy (those with an interest in maintaining the rewards of capital) are weak. The central preoccupation of policy is then reduced to being a matter of controlling the pace of retreat. The aim becomes the negative one of trying to prevent the whole system blowing up in an orgy of state and private consumption, leaving a nil return to the instruments of capital, with all income being distributed through the interplay of trade union power and rival political and bureaucratic pressures. Keynes in the Concluding Notes to the *General Theory* set out his 'civilized' version of controlling this situation, in which clever and disinterested public servants in authority would somehow be able to hold the ring in the face of all these pressures. They would do the investing. Consumption would be dutifully constrained.

In the post-war period with the pay 'tiger' out of its cage, attempts to control the pace and prevent the 'orgy' have employed a succession of incomes policies. While they are in operation the shift is momentarily slowed. When they collapse it moves rapidly ahead again. That is the unstable path Britain has been on and it is this which leads many economists to predict the blow-up, the ultimate clash between unleashed collective 'bargaining' and resources which are not there and are not being generated.

The fundamental question therefore is whether we can see a way ahead which preserves, indeed strengthens, the position of capital while recognizing the economic requirement for a widespread distribution of purchasing power and the political pressures that go with it. This is what a possible fourth type of capitalism — the capitalism of the future — seeks to meet. The basic argument is straightforward. If ownership of capital is widespread then the political penalties on capital returns cease to be a 'popular' cause and become an unpopular one. The pressures go into reverse. The demands for a higher 'share' for labour, whether through union pressure or state taxation and redistribution — fuelled by competitive vote-bidding — are in large part replaced by demands for fairer returns on capital and a better income for the masses who own capital.

It requires no vast political insight to see that if society can move only a modest way in this direction some at least of the apparently irreconcilable tensions of welfare capitalism will be eased and a new political interest established (or, it could be argued, an old one re-established). First, this new pattern of capitalism relies upon *diffused* ownership, which provides in-built political support for property rights and property respect *and* a permanent check on the conglomeration of both economic and political power in the hands of modern Government.

Second, this new capitalism, because it is widespread, dilutes and in fact largely removes the master-servant, two-class relationship built into other forms of capitalism. The contrast is especially great with the pattern of state capitalism, which requires a very powerful ruling political and economic class, controlling all the property, to decide who should get what income, or, in other words, what people's 'needs' really are.

Third, a capitalist system based on far wider diffusion of capital, and of income from capital, breaks the dominating conceptual link between employment and livelihood which is at the centre both of 'full employment' economic orthodoxy and much contemporary mythology about the way workers are supposed to live and what they are supposed to want.

The traditional case for governments trying to pursue full employment policies had *four* major orthodox underpinnings: (a) it was the only means by which most people could bring an income into households; (b) it was necessary in order to generate sufficient mass purchasing power to prevent depression; (c) it was necessary to maintain high production; and (d) it was necessary to social stability to have everybody occupied.

Welfare capitalism obviously invalidates the first of these arguments. Every family now receives weekly child credits, for example. But a capitalism based on really broad capital ownership overtakes all three of them. It does so because the wide distribution of ownership means that millions of families acquire an income pattern previously believed to be confined to the better off, i.e. *a second income* from personal capital accumulated to supplement wages or salary. Of course it may be that this second income is taken out in the form of leisure, as in the case of a self-employed person or small businessman who finds he can get more time off, or hire someone to mind the shop. But the principle is the same and it is, of course, a principle already widely practised.

Moreover, while it is true that only a small minority of families in Britain today receive income from investments of a size sufficient to constitute a significant part of the weekly income, a very large number receive a second income of a different kind – in the form of direct subventions from the state. In other words, for very large numbers a single remunerated employment is *no longer* the only means of livelihood or the only source of family income.

As for employment being necessary to production, here too, the realities already confronting us show this not to be so. In fact, the problem is now to find something to do for the growing numbers displaced by technology. Production does not require them. Nor does the imperative of mass purchasing power, if that purchasing power is placed in many hands through other channels – at present through welfare redistribution which puts purchasing power in the hands of families *irrespective* of employment, or through the maintenance or creation of non-productive jobs on a large-scale, as a means of getting purchasing power spread around.

There is lastly the question of being occupied, either because idle hands make mischief, or because lack of occupation is boring or debilitating or unfulfilling. Let us accept all these as perfectly valid reasons for trying to see that everyone is occupied. But does that mean that they must be employed? The mythology naturally answers 'yes' since the assumption is built into it that the living wage and the occupation go together.

Remove that assumption and we have a world much closer to the real one of today than class politicians care to admit. A typical family income now might have four components – one, regular wages from some fixed weekly employment in industry; two, benefit income through family credits, assuming there are children, and quite possibly through other forms of state support as well; three, income from part-time work, maybe a bit of self-employment, helping a neighbour in exchange for goods in kind or skills offered in return and, four, from the wife's earnings (over half of all married women now being out at work).

The untypical fifth source of income might be a bit of interest from National Savings or Building Society deposits or a bit of rent from the lodger. The very untypical fifth source would be a substantial income, say over £20 a week, from savings. Inland Revenue figures suggest that in 1976-77 4.8 per cent of 'tax units' showed investment income of over £20 per week. But of course this takes no account of families with more than one tax unit − i.e. where the wife is taxed separately.

Now, all this is noticeably removed from the simple romance of the worker and his regular industrial employment versus the boss and his capital and his leisure (particularly since the boss or manager in this case may be no nearer ownership than the employee).

Moreover, in a technically advanced economy it could well be the regular employment component of the weekly occupation pattern I have outlined which is most at risk. So the next question is this. What if the regular job goes, if the worker is replaced by a machine or a silicon chip or a new, labour-saving technique, introduced either in his own firm, or in some other firm, with resulting loss of orders to his firm and therefore loss of jobs, including his own?

The conventional answer for post-war policy-makers has been that one of two things must happen. Either the government uses taxation taken from the wage or salary to support employment levels in the affected firm or firms, in which case the affected worker will receive what is in effect a state income at one remove. Or he will go unemployed and receive a similar income direct from the state. Either way he will now be getting a chunk of his livelihood from something other than genuine productive employment, although he and his wife may still be picking up some income on other odd and part-time jobs. If he is officially unemployed he will have 'leisure' which he can use as he wishes. Maybe, if the mood takes him and demoralization can be overcome he will help with local voluntary work, or organize the local, model aero club, or use the opportunity to read history or listen to classical music or paint the house or join evening classes or garden or get to know the children better or look after them more, while the other partner spends more time on her job or one of a dozen other occupations.

So *superficially*, there is no reason why a worker should be *unoccupied*, as distinct from unemployed, except by choice. And nor, at first glance, is there any reason why he should be living very differently from someone who is getting precisely the same income from capital assets rather than from the fortnightly unemployment benefit cheque. In another age, that, after all, was the preferred living pattern of the rentier class.

But, of course, in reality there is all the difference in the world between the two situations. One way is impermanent, dependent, unsettling and, to many people, undignified. The other way is enduring, independent and liberating. One way is by courtesy of 'them', the assessors of need, the bureaucracy, the new class. It carries the unemployment stigma. The other way is by right, by courtesy of no official. One way pushes a man into the economic wilderness, the other way embraces him within society and gives him a stable status within the system.

Kelso puts the point this rather blunt way.

Unemployment, in short, is natural and desirable in technically advanced economies. The task of capitalist economies is not to fight unemployment at *any* cost, like the plague. Rather its objectives should be to make certain that normal technological unemployment falls upon thos who can afford it, and to whom it should be the greatest of blessings.

This may seem an extraordinary, even outrageous viewpoint. How, it will be asked, can anyone possibly 'afford' unemployment? Should not policy-makers be straining every sinew to come up with ideas for keeping people in work, preserving jobs, sharing jobs, subsidizing jobs, especially in manufacturing industry, where the labour force is shrinking so fast?

But if the real concern is with livelihood and a busy, full life, rather than with employment as an end in itself, should we be so nervous about seeing things this way? There is, in any case the still small voice of realism on the employment question. And realism tells us that from now on, in a society like ours, the employment situation, at least in manufacturing, is going to get very much tougher. Third and Fourth World competition, together with advanced technology, signal shrinking numbers in manufacturing, at least in the traditional areas such as heavy engineering, steel shipbuilding and the mass production goods such as cars and consumer machinery generally.

This does not mean to say that all those displaced will 'inevitably' be without remunerated work. There is no 'fixed' amount of work to be done in a creative and civilized society. We do not need to fall victim to the 'lump of labour' fallacy or, as Samuel Brittan puts it, to the 'outrageous absurdity' of the thinking which colours much official and union utterances on the employment future. [6]

What it certainly does mean is that the typical household income is going to change shape, that there will be less certainty of regular weekly wages from factory work and a growing tendency − unless policy-makers frustrate it − to combine the maintenance of the weekly income with increased leisure.

How is this pattern going to be financed? The policy-makers of the Left have an easy answer to that one. Either the state will pay, or benefits will be raised to pay for earlier retirement and longer schooling, or public sector non-jobs must be expanded dramatically, or employers must be required to pay the same for substantially fewer hours worked, which eventually works through in lower productivity and lower real wages.

In these ways everyone will be kept in an occupation of sorts and everyone, in left-wing theory at any rate, will be happy. There is no doubt that this is the course upon which Britain has been drifting. And of course there are two colossal penalties that have to be paid for going this way.

The first is that the power of state and union officials grows exorbitantly. A vast and expanding redistributive machinery is required to pay out the incomes of an increasing proportion of the population in accordance with state-decided and union-decided priorities. The occupation pattern ceases to have any direct relation with economic and productive requirements and becomes instead a centrally-determined order. A 'labouristic' distribution of income then prevails.

Second, the income to finance this 'pocket-money society' has to be raised by taxing the wealth-creators at levels so high that the incentive to wealth-creation − i.e. to new capital formation − is eventually undermined.

The pattern is therefore set for impoverishment and state dominance. It is inherently politically unstable, and, with the shrinkage of traditional industrial employment, it is given a new and accelerated force − unless, of course, we are prepared to go along new conceptual paths and adopt new priorities.

Earlier (see chapter 5) reference was made to Prof. J. K. Galbraith's hope that this new path could be charted by a wise and 'emancipated' legislature, which would control and own a substantial part of the capital structure of the economy and would see that income and the resources of the state were 're-directed' in accordance with the public interest.[7]

Galbraith was really doing no more than trying to find a plausible American replacement for the assumptions upon which Keynes was able gracefully to rest his own beliefs, namely that 'the state' would behave in an enlightened way in carrying out the role of management, investment and redistribution assigned to it in the General Theory. Full employment would unify and stabilize the nation. Economic decision-making could be insulated from political pressures and reserved for the attentions of educated administrators and experts.

Keynes could believe this in the thirties because that was the way his world worked. A marvellously civilized and unprejudiced civil service still reigned in Whitehall. The Bank of England still controlled monetary policy. The political Left was not dominant in the Labour Party and the unions were still living under the shadow of 1926. Organized collectivist political power was not yet in a position, either in the unions or in the administration, to seize hold of the controls and turn up the inflationary heat. Mild income redistribution could be confidently left to the state to undertake.

In this kind of world it seemed safe to assume that ownership of the instruments of production was indeed a matter of minor consequence. In the 1950s Anthony Crosland was still asserting the same belief.[8] But that is not what the political Left in the Labour Party or the unions believed and not what they have practised. For them ownership is the vital issue. Its possession by the state at the centre gives the new class power and its diffusion weakens that power. This is the point that the bourgeois intellect understood as well as the Marxist intellect. The tragedy is that it was hidden so long from the minds of well-meaning administrators in Britain, as well as their liberal admirers in America, whose forbears would have understood all about the deeply stabilizing influence of the ownership factor, but who themselves had forgotten, or buried in deliberate expiation of past, middle-class sins, this fundamentally important ideal.

The alternative to the state 'solutions' of Keynes and of

Galbraith rests in a pattern of *diffused*, instead of centralized, capital ownership. And at the heart of this alternative lies the concept of *a second income* for each family, based not on a central conception of need but on capital individually owned. By this is meant the idea that most families should be either in the position, or moving upwards towards the position, in which personal income from owned capital sources becomes a substantial factor in the weekly household income, a permanent and secure supplement to the less certain wage or salary. Thus the more leisured pattern wanted by the visionaries would begin to be financed without unceasing calls for more state aid.

It is true that many households today have long since taken hold of the second income concept in one form or another. There is the rapidly-growing tendency for both partners in a marriage to go out to work. And there is the enormous growth of the moonlighting 'second' economy. Both are understandable but neither is intrinsically good. The both-out-to-work arrangement too often takes father and mother away from the family at once. The household budget may be nicely reinforced but at a heavy price in other ways. As for moonlighting, while present tax levels make it inevitable, it is bound to breed a subterranean culture of dishonesty and disunity (and is already doing so).

The second income for which families are evidently looking should surely come not from these measures of desperation but from the ownership of income-producing capital assets. Many forms of self-employment go half-way along this path. 'Capital' in the form of goodwill is built up, or a corner shop is purchased, or a garage franchise, enabling the capital-owner, in theory at any rate, to work less than the full nine-to-five 'eyes down' routine and still have a living. Of course it does not always work that way, as many struggling self-employed people well know. But the possibility of a second-income-supported existence is there, and this is a trend which obviously fits in with the work arrangements of the future — which is why education and training programmes ought to put far more emphasis on training for self-employment and 'running your own show' than they do.

In other words the pattern of the future will combine a whole range of different forms of ownership − through self-employment, partial- or full-time, through small business ownership, through industrial share ownership and through asset- and property-ownership.

The question is how policies ought to be shaped and adapted to fit this new environment, and how attitudes deeply embedded in existing policies which constantly drive against and frustrate these trends can be removed.

What we now require is an approach which coaxes and encourages workers to move out of the age of wage-subservience and into an age of ownership and independence. It is along this path that the way lies, away from the explosive wage pressures which Keynesian demand-management could not contain and from which monetarism by itself, while it provides the necessary financial framework, cannot protect modern society.

In the next chapter I set out the essentials of this approach and describe the point of departure for the policies needed to bring the greater political and economic stability which still seems to be eluding us.

CHAPTER 8

Measures and Money

A time there was, ere England's griefs began,
When every rood of ground maintained its man.
Oliver Goldsmith *The Deserted Village*

The changes in our society, outlined in earlier chapters will be
hastened − or at least not hindered − by policies and
measures which can be grouped under the following five
headings:

(1) The introduction of policies to allow the creation of
numerous new capitalist enterprises, and thus to broaden and
decentralize the country's business and industrial structure.

(2) Measures to broaden the ownership of existing
enterprises, especially through employee ownership and other
wider ownership schemes in both the private and public
sectors.

(3) Financial and tax policies aimed at introducing millions
more families into the 'ownership' part of society.

(4) Measures designed to increase, rather than suppress,
awareness of the degree to which mass ownership of the
capital instruments of production in the economy already
exists, and to strengthen that sense of ownership.

(5) The replacement of policies which encourage impersonal
industrial concentration in state and institutional hands with
policies which counter-balance these tendencies and which

lead to a more dispersed and diffused pattern of economic power into smaller industrial units.

In chapter 5 some changes in the conduct of industrial policy were proposed which would help to create these conditions. But we must now go further, although, one of the main dangers in filling out the details of such a programme must be acknowledged right away. It lies in the tendency to end up either with a 'solution' so miraculously all-curative that it sounds ridiculous, or with a rag bag of minor changes and adjustments which does not sound like a recognizable programme at all.

For example, employee share ownership schemes – about which we shall have a good deal to say – undoubtedly have a very important part to play in broadening capital ownership. But we must be careful to avoid the impression given by some enthusiasts that this kind of direct leap from non-ownership into full equity ownership provides a surefire method of achieving mass capitalism which should be universally applied. It may well be wiser and more realistic to think of the ownership idea as spreading outwards through the modern commnity in ripples, with some measures designed near the centre to restore the attractiveness of direct equity holding for medium-size investors, who are already at home with the principles of asset ownership, and other measures tailored for those much further removed from any kind of previous contact with capitalist concepts. For example, bonds with a limited risk element might be a better starting point for this latter category.

The aim must be to acquaint a very large number of earners and their families with the idea of ownership in some form, well down the scale from risk-bearing equities. The point is that a well-thought out programme must seek to cater for people at *all* stages of understanding of, and familiarity with, the personal ownership idea. Each group has to be encouraged to come one stage forward towards greater participation than before in the ownership of the nation's wealth and the capital instruments which generate future capital and income.

A second point is that the concern here is not with increasing the level of savings but increasing the extent of *ownership*. The two obviously overlap in the sense that a pound saved in any medium is a pound owned. Any act of saving is obviously a welcome, if small, move up the stairway from total dependence on the weekly wage to a more stable and secure situation.

But it is the extent to which this process heightens the sense of ownership of a share in the nation's productive capacity which interess us most of all, so that if National Savings are better than nothing, and unit trusts are better than that, and bonds or debentures are better again, a direct equity holding is the most telling and direct form of ownership of industry of all.

If it was just a question of raising the level of savings then Britain would compare quite favourably with other nations. It is true that the level of personal savings as a proportion of personal disposable income has been running at somewhat lower levels here than in, say, West Germany, although according to a recent comparative study of saving and investment in Britain and West Germany, the gap has closed considerably in recent years.[1]

But Britain undoubtedly has a very wide range of savings incentives and outlets. Indeed, due to features in the tax system, which give very large reliefs for some forms of savings, (notably through pension schemes and life assurance schemes), and for the proceeds of those savings, and no reliefs for other forms at all, the variety of savings media and the number of 'incentives' has long since become bewilderingly complex.

However, the real issue is how these arrangements help towards the objective of wider personal ownership, and here the contrast with other free countries is much more telling.

For example, West German policy has been strenuously concerned, from the earliest days of post-war reconstruction, with the encouragement of personal wealth accumulation among an ever-widening stratum of society. The openly recognized objective has been to move towards a much more widely dispersed and equal pattern of ownership of the nation's productive property in order to strengthen political support for the institution of private property. 'The country's secret weapon against Communism' was how post-war German leaders described this strategy and this underlying attitude has clearly heavily influenced the country's whole approach to the promotion of savings in the post-war years. 'Property-holding', Konrad Adenauer told his party, 'is one of the essential safeguards of the democratic state'.[2]

This attitude comes out strongly in the idea of the 'investment wage' and in the various provisions under the Wealth Accumulation Laws (Vermogensbildungsgesetze), introduced from the early sixties onwards to carry the whole cause rapidly forward. It is reflected too in the so-called Friedrichs-Schiller plan and its many variants – this being a set of measures aimed at encouraging direct share investment schemes for employees. And we get the same story from the very prominent place which schemes of ownership promotion have been given in the deliberations of the Council of Experts on Economic Development – the driving body in West Germany's 'concerted action' arrangements. The idea of the investment 'wage' is simply that the employer pays a slice of the weekly or monthly total remuneration into a special investment account belonging to the employee, where it sits and attracts any one of a wide variety of tax privileges, allowances or direct subsidy premiums, paid direct from the state, according to circumstances.

The theory is breathtakingly simple, perhaps a bit too simple. It is that while the extra resources paid out by companies for the investment wage, on top of normal wages, obviously eat into profits, the company, when it wants to invest and expand, can then go to the bank holding the accumulated investment wages and borrow them back on attractive terms. In other words, internal or auto-finance is replaced by finance linked to employee ownership and involvement. Equity is built into the workers.

In practice things have certainly not worked as smoothly as this. Not all firms are in the happy position of contemplating expansion, however financed. For some, the only thing the investment wage means is just another burden on industrial costs with no foreseeable compensatory advantages. Nonetheless, the major German unions approached the idea constructively and by the end of the sixties about 6.5 million workers had negotiated agreements which included some form of investment wage. By 1973 Samuels and McMahon (in their comparative study for the Anglo-German Foundation)[3] estimated that the number involved had risen to 13 million.

On top of this the same authors estimate that there are about 2,000 West German firms operating full-blooded employee share schemes. A further mass of reliefs and state credits help to promote house purchase and home improvement.

All this does not necessarily add up to a neat pattern under which the average German worker feels himself to be a middle-class capital owner. The situation is very far from that. In fact, Dr George Copeman, author of the remarkable book *Employee Share Ownership and Industrial Stability*[4] estimates that only about 6.8 per cent of Germans of working age and above own shares, as against a figure of roughly 3.8 per cent in Britain, 9.8 per cent in France and 20.5 per cent in the United States.

But it does, nevertheless, ensure that for millions of German families the 'modified' capitalist system, operating on social market principles, means something very direct and beneficial. This is quite different from saying that West Germany is an individualist's paradise full of mini-capitalists all doing their own thing. On the contrary, these arrangements appear to go hand in hand with a remarkable degree of social cohesion and readiness to see work and business as a group or team undertaking, demanding close involvement by all members.

We have here an example of the personal ownership *paradox*. The more fragmented, dispersed, widely-shared the ownership pattern in a society, through worker shareholdings or family business, the greater the sense of common cause; and the greater the desire tends to be to pitch together. The more diffuse the power, the greater the unity. The converse of this is that the tighter the control along centralist and collectivist principles, the greater the tensions, the alienation and the divisive pressures.

I shall return to this paradox in a moment, but before doing so, I want to take a look at our nearest continental neighbour, France. The French, too, have plunged with enthusiasm into the cause of mass-ownership in the post-war years. Here too, as in West Germany, political idealism has been well to the fore, with the result that the hard practical details of spreading ownership have not always had the attention they require. In 1967 a Gaullist decree, introduced in the sweeping manner which is born of grandeur and has no time for petty matters of detail, laid down that all firms with over one hundred employees should be required to introduce deferred profit-sharing schemes, the profit being locked in for employees and invested either in the company's own shares or in the stock market for a fixed number of years before full vesting in the employee's possession.

This was followed in 1970 by an even more ambitious proposal diverting nationalized undertakings, including Renault and certain state banks and insurance companies, to distribute shares to employees. Most of these schemes have made very slow progress, but the Renault example is especially interesting because it is attempting to disperse the largest concentration of all, the state-owned sector.

There are two very significant points here. First, the very idea of wishing to disperse state-owned assets into the workers' hands embodies a refutation of the doctrine that state ownership *is* public ownership and that nationalized undertakings already 'belong to the workers'. This confusion is at the heart of much British political thinking and it is fascinating to see how a nation like France, which has retained in its public consciousness an understanding of the real meaning of property ownership, is able to go right past this facade and make public policy which acknowledges the true nature of state ownership and its inherent inferiority to personal ownership on a mass scale.

The second important point is that French policy-makers have been prepared actually to do something about their beliefs. The air of hopelessness in British politics in the seventies, mentioned in earlier chapters, stemmed at least in part from the fear that state enlargement is a one-way process, and that no schemes for dispersing this enormous and growing economic power could ever be 'on' politically or workable in practice. The French plan for Renault shows a quite different spirit. Initially, five per cent of the company's shares have been distributed on a basis of earnings and length of service. But the aim is to take the individual share holding as high as twenty-five per cent, leaving seventy-five per cent in state hands.

Of course there is no reason why dispersal should stop at this point. Many major companies survive and prosper without anybody holding a controlling block of shares. If the assets of the enterprise really *are* assets (i.e. if the enterprise is making a profit on capital invested) there is no good reason why those assets should not be progressively transferred to a variety of non-state forms of ownership, although it may be, as George Copeman has suggested, that for the employees of a particular enterprise to own more than twenty-five per cent raises problems of influence and control which are better avoided. [5]

But either way, the French readiness to grapple with state ownership is vastly encouraging. All the arguments against excessive concentration of economic power and against the divided character which this gives any society apply tenfold where the power is the state. It is, in Copeman's phrase 'the worst absentee owner of all'. [6]

Very recently, the French have again sought to take the

principle of mass ownership further forward. The centrepiece of the new programme has been a tax relief allowing private individuals in France to deduct up to Fr. 5,000 a year from their income, free of tax, provided it is invested either in the French equivalent of unit trusts or in French equities. These new stimuli come on top of existing provisions developed from the original Gaullist ideas to give further encouragement to companies to distribute capital to employees and also on top of extensive provisions giving tax relief on the first slice of income from investments (up to about Fr. 3,000).

These measures have been accompanied by commitments by French Government Ministers to the goal of broadened ownership and greater 'reconciliation' between France and its industry. The results appear to have been quite dramatic, vastly increasing the number of direct shareholders and, incidentally, breathing new life into the stockmarket.

Then, there is the vastly different situation of the United States. America's historical roots lie in a mass distribution of small parcels of property so that the whole culture continues to be as favourable to the wide spread of property in its modern capitalist guise as the British culture is unfavourable. Ninety per cent of companies listed on the New York Stock Exchange run stock option schemes, while 200,000 companies run profit-sharing schemes of one kind or another. American industry bristles with thrift plans, stock bonus plans, and profit-sharing plans, although it should be appreciated that some of these are in lieu of pension plans. All in all, America today, despite continuing vast concentrations of capital, is the nearest thing that exists to a popular capitalist society. The American legislature is deeply committed to the promotion of wider ownership, as one would expect in a nation with strong traditions of populist politics.

In Britain, Dr George Copeman has developed similar ideas. Dismissing some of the central fallacies which govern popular thinking about the way wealth is accumulated,

Copeman argues for a wide range of policy changes which would accelerate the involvement by millions of wage earners in direct share ownership and in the capital formation process. His thinking played a large part in the scheme put forward first by the Conservative Party in 1976 for tax encouragement to employee share ownership[7] and subsequently in the provisions in Labour's 1978 Finance Act which gave limited tax reliefs on payments in the form of deferred profit shares made by companies to their workers.

What, then, are the possibilities for Britain across this whole field in the immediate future? The characteristics of 'ownership' in Britain from which we have to start are broadly these:

(1)   A very low proportion of direct equity holding and a low involvement generally in the financial mechanisms which determine the pattern of ownership in the country.

(2)   A wide variety of savings schemes, as numerous as those available in neighbouring free countries, most of them built round a complicated system of tax reliefs. These reliefs affect both money saved out of income and the consequent income from savings only to a minor extent. Their chief feature is the advantage they give to contractual saving through pension plans and, to a slightly lesser extent, through life assurance.

(3)   A relatively few company-wide share schemes (about one hundred). Of these much the best known and most often quoted is the ICI scheme but several other very well-known companies operate share schemes and there are also share plans operated by unquoted companies, again embracing all employees.

(4)   Virtually no concern in tax policies or other public policy for the idea of broadening the distribution of wealth, and almost complete disinterest in the argument that a wider distribution of *wealth* might reduce pressures for the attempted redistribution of *income* through staggeringly high income tax rates and a complex pattern of state benefits.

(5) A relatively high degree of home ownership overall (higher in fact than in France) largely achieved during the boom in home ownership in the 1950s, with an uneasy truce since then between a large ownership sector and an almost equally large public authority housing sector especially concentrated in Scotland and The North East, the private rented sector being squeezed to a sliver in between.

(6) A heavy concentration of industrial ownership in state, and to a lesser extent in private hands, with a noticeably smaller number of people employed in the independent sector and in family businesses than in Germany, France, America or Japan.[1] According to Dr S. J. Prais of the National Institute of Economic and Social Research thirty per cent of the US *manufacturing* labour force is still engaged in firms with less than 200 employees, while the figure for the UK is twenty per cent. This takes no account of the much more developed service sector in the United States where, of course, smaller firms and self-employment predominate.

(7) An ethos in industry which tends to be deeply hostile to ideas of working together, seeking common cause and commitment to the team production effort. This is because the whole traditional culture cries out that there are divided interests, with capital lined up on one side and labour on the other.

The starting point for a change in the British climate towards ownership has to be in tax policy and in the enormous disincentives to private share ownership. A general lowering of the tax rate, particularly as it affects incomes, will have two decisive effects. It will increase the incentive to use savings for the acquisition of income – generating assets – and it will reduce the relative attraction of putting all savings into the pension or the life policy.

There can be no doubt that such a change would be thoroughly healthy and greatly to the benefit of the pension funds and insurance institutions themselves. The continuation of trends towards investment dominance by the institutions can only have two very undesirable consequences. The first is the growth in the proportion of investment decisions which are, in effect, committee-based rather than entrepreneur-driven. Admittedly, that is a trend which some large institutions, and large firms, are trying hard to overcome by devising special programmes to encourage investment in smaller enterprises. But large institutions cannot be expected to invest below a certain level of size. They cannot back the one-man business or finance the corner shop. The second consequence is the attraction of much facile comment about the activities of the pension and insurance institutions, ranging from demands that they should somehow be more accountable to various constituencies (the contributors, the other shareholders in the enterprises where they own large blocks, the firms they control, the public, Parliament, etc.), to outright proposals for takeover by collectivist bodies such as the trade union movement (or rather its officials), or the state.

In the 1977 Conservative Party document, 'The Right Approach to the Economy',[8] some of my colleagues and I set out the main features of a comprehensive programme of tax reform and reduction. This involved attacking the ridiculously high marginal income tax rates, modifying the capital taxes, easing the burden of the investment income surcharge and cutting the standard rate of income tax.

This is the right way to start. But it would be good to see things taken much further in due course – a possibility which looks infinitely more promising in combination with a progressive broadening in the capital ownership structure than in the present climate of hostility to capital.

In reality there is no reason at all why Britain should be forever a high tax country, and in particular a country with almost uniquely high taxes of earning and wealth accumulation. The mood has grown up that somehow it will always be so, just as the mood has grown up that we are doomed to live with, and accept, the trade union veto on business and commercial expansion and to build all 'realistic' public policy around this gloomy assumption. But it need not be so. And the wider spread of capital ownership would give policy-makers the confidence to see that it need not be so.

Beyond the tax cuts outlined in Conservative policy documents in the late seventies, a possibility in this area might be to devise tax reliefs available to all income earners, allowing a substantial first slice of income to be set aside, tax free, and invested in equities or appropriate unit trusts. This would be in line with the French schemes already mentioned.

Moving beyond tax reduction, the aim must be to spread employee share ownership much faster. For a start, there is room to build on the very modest scheme of incentive for employee share ownership schemes in the 1978 Finance Act, although many firms will want to develop their own variants of this idea. [9]

Nicholas Goodison, the Chairman of the London Stock Exchange, and a ceaseless campaigner for much wider ownership of capital, was probably right when he argued that this legislation did not go far enough. [10] For one thing, the limit of £500 a year which the Government places on the value of the shares which may be handed to the employee without attracting full income tax is much too small. For another, the employee has to wait up to ten years to be free of income tax completely and this seems much too long. The French scheme introduced by de Gaulle twenty years ago allowed complete freedom from income tax after five years. A third major weakness is that the legislation prevents companies from distributing shares in subsidiaries or associates and, even more serious, it excludes companies or organizations in the public sector which might want to operate profit-sharing or bonus-sharing schemes with an 'ownership' element in them. In such cases there would be no tax benefit at all.

We should follow the French lead with Renault and devise schemes for diluting concentrated state ownership of nationalized industries. The poor past performance of some of the state industries obviously limits what can be done immediately in the way of distributing shares which have any value, future or current. But schemes have now been developed which go some way to meeting this difficulty, and of either privatizing or partially introducing private ownership, possibly on a wide scale in the state-owned sector.

An even more diverting scheme, for diffusing the benefits of North Sea Oil, has been proposed by Samuel Brittan.[11] His idea is that the total revenues arising from North Sea Oil extraction should be distributed on a '*pro rata*' basis to all UK citizens. These payments would be in the form of transferable rights and would therefore have a capital value and be marketable. Thus North Sea Oil stock would be a powerful medium for carrying the 'message' of capital ownership to millions of people over a fairly short period. Brittan has even proposed a modification which would overcome the disadvantage that North Sea Oil is a wasting asset. Thus, the twenty or thirty years of life in the North Sea Oil wells would pave the way to a permanent layer of equity ownership in Britain, giving the country a new source of stability and unity over the next century, long after the fossil fuel itself has been mined.

Some people have argued for the setting up of a single, vast kind of unit trust, on the lines of the 'workers fund' proposed by the Swedish trade union organizations, on the grounds that this would enlarge worker ownership of industry. But it does not seem to me that this would deepen and strengthen the idea and feeling of ownership in any way at all. The 'ownership' would be remote and indirect. There would be no sense of personal possession and personal involvement at all. Pension funds and insurance companies have their place in organizing the pensions and security they were set up to provide, and in doing so they offer an element of indirect ownership. But the need is for something more tangible than this and certainly much more intimate than any great public unit trust could engender. It is *direct* ownership which is required and which should be fostered, both by changes in the conduct of public policy outlined in earlier chapters and by the kind of tax-encouraged schemes mentioned here.

If, over the next few years, the policy-makers embark step by step on a strategy which contains these main elements, and if these measures are combined with the change of direction in industrial and social policies proposed elsewhere in this essay, then it is perfectly possible that a very rapid change in the economic, social and political landscape in Britain will occur. This will be not so much through the power of these policies to act positively on the economy, as through their capacity to release and channel a potential which is *already there* and, I believe, growing all the time.

But for this to happen the attitudes of the past so prevalent in the policy-making establishment must be altered mightily. Their thinking must cease to be influenced so overwhelmingly by class 'fears' and the stereotyped views that go with such fears, and begin to be influenced by a very different set of values, hopes and judgments about the shape of the democratic future. The myth that share ownership is only for the rich, not for the workers, must be systematically exposed and destroyed, just as the myth that only the rich own their own homes has *been* destroyed.

Let it be clear that this is not just another cry for individualism in a world of big battalions. That is brave but impractical. The modern version of the old bourgeois ethic is just as much coloured by belief in community, in mutual obligation, in interdependent teamwork, as was the old order. Indeed it is more so, since modern business operations so obviously involve a much more complicated pattern of mutual dependence between the services and skills involved than the simpler world of Adam Smith.

My theme, therefore, cannot be simply labelled 'free market' or 'individualist'. It fits into an age where men and women may be reacting against remote centralism and bureaucratic pyramids of power and privilege, but where they still seek security on common ground and through common bonds. It also fits in with today's Conservative Party and the mood and character that has now settled over that Party. How that has come about, where this places Conservatives today in the political spectrum and how our political institutions will cope with these great changes, will be the subject of the concluding chapters.

CHAPTER 9

Another Britain

Corporate bodies have no souls.
Attributed to Lord Thurlow
and quoted by William Hazlitt

As I argued earlier, the popular rejection of the old corporate order, and the political arrangements and attitudes that go with it, can and will take highly dangerous forms for a society which is unprepared for the change. No more spectacular example of this can be found than in the recent experience of the British trade union movement, which behind an appearance of venerable and monolithic power and unity has seen its influence weakened by a thousand splinter groups, each determined to pursue its grievances remorselessly and pay no more than nominal allegiance to higher authority.

This is the risk which liberal politicians taken when they persistently overrate collectivist and class sentiments. The deeper, and in the end, more powerful instincts against block conformity and impersonal size find a new and dangerous way out. Politics and parliamentary method can then offer no road back, for they, too, are discredited. Just as in 1978 desperate attempts by the fading Labour Government to restore the authority of official trade union institutions by more political concessions provided no road back from the fragmentation and near-anarchy into which organized labour was drifting.

The same process has been taking place in a wider political sphere. It is not just the institution of centralized trade unionism which is falling apart. On all sides views are now being pressed for constitutional reform, for Parliamentary reform, for electoral reform, some muddled and self-defeating, some well-directed. Scarcely a week goes by without a new group coming out with a study or report on possible constitutional change. A strong and active lobby for changing the electoral system from first past the post to proportional representation has grown up. Parliamentary reform groups proliferate and the issue is constantly aired in Parliament. Lords reform is on the agenda. The Scottish and Welsh devolution causes were undoubtedly part of the same movement when they began to become prominent, although in the hands of the old policy-making establishment they have long since become mutated and distorted into schemes for more centralism, not less, and for a further concentration of power in bureaucratic hands rather than a diffusion of power to the people.

All this marks a great change, compared with the situation as recently as ten years ago. It is true that in the late sixties the devolution impulses were beginning and Lords reform was being attempted. But interest in Parliamentary reform was minimal and the idea that the House of Commons might ever be restored as a decisive influence on policy was barely entertained. Those who aired such ideas were branded as hopelessly unrealistic. Did they not understand that there was a great ideological battle to be fought out, a struggle between capital and labour, which the two major parties were in Parliament to wage?

When I published a pamphlet at the end of the sixties attempting to link the case for radical Parliamentary reform with reform of the whole bureaucratic machine and the Whitehall Departments, my discussion of the machinery received some attention but few seemed interested in the Parliamentary part.[1] I tried there to explain that better focused Parliamentary scrutiny of both policy manufacture and execution in Whitehall was a vital part of the reform programme, without which the whole structure of reform fell, and that a Parliament preoccupied with fighting the class war would do nothing at all to change the stereotyped attitudes which underlay Whitehall policy-making.

Along with tight overall control on Government spending (also something of an absent guest after 1972) it seemed to me that Parliamentary influence, through strong and informed committees, was the other arch of the edifice. Without it, no attempts to question, challenge or terminate unnecessary departmental procedures and policies could ever be pressed home. Ministers were few whilst public servants were many. Without outside political push every endeavour could be safely diverted into a review body or study group which might drag on for years and which Ministers could not hope to follow in detail, let alone attend.

It is true that this was the period when the old Estimates Committees were wound up and the new umbrella Expenditure Committee set up in its place. But one only had to hear some of the 'wise' comments on this change to realize that its chances of sparking a revived Parliamentary contribution to the control of the Executive were virtually nil. For most, except a few enthusiasts, it was no more than another way of keeping idle hands out of mischief, 'giving backbenchers something to do'. The idea that the backbenchers of the House of Commons could play a key part in lifting public policy out of the rut, and actually helping Government move the debate on, simply did not enter the reckoning.

In *The Dilemma of Democracy* published in 1978, Lord Hailsham came at these questions another way.[2] He argued that the problem lay in an 'elective dictatorship', the product of a two party Parliamentary system, based on single-member constituencies, which allowed the party with a bare majority to dictate the whole policy pattern. Lord Hailsham claimed that this allowed violent swings in public policy to take place, even when there had been a barely perceptible shift in public opinion. Means had to be sought of bringing more balance into the party political set-up in the House of Commons.

This led him to examine sympathetically the idea of a change to proportional representation as a way of thwarting dictatorial party rule by either side, and of restoring a pattern of limited government, operating under the rule of law.

But does the problem really lie in 'party' and 'party government'? Surely when there are broadly shared assumptions about the shape of society and its values, the swings of fortune in Parliament leading to a change of team from time to time without a great revolution in public opinion is an excellent thing? It allows a fresh lot to try their hand without enormous doctrinal upheaval and has at times undoubtedly worked very well.

What wrecks it all is the introduction of class politics on to the scene, infecting all the political parties and turning the normal party majority, whether drawn from one party or several, into what Lord Hailsham describes as a dictatorial grouping.

Nor am I certain about the great swings of policy that are alleged to have taken place between Governments in the post-war years. Swings of rhetoric there may have been, swings certainly of Ministerial intention. But in practice the main components of policy have so far remained pretty well unchanged. The policy-makers look at the Parliamentary scene, study their social surveys and carry on with the same broad lines of policy, righteously convinced of their own realism and of their own 'balanced' view that the only sensible choice lies in for ever walking the tightrope between appeasement and confrontation of a mighty working class, whose existence and power is held to be unquestionable. It could well be argued that the swing really needed in policy, away from the capital-versus-labour false perspective, is the one that has not regrettably taken place.

Looked at this way it becomes very hard to see how a change to proportional representation would help things one way or another. As long as the 'Two-Nations' complex clouded political thinking, as long as it was believed that the key to sound policy lay with trade union officialdom and its demands, all that a Government could do was to walk down the middle of this old familiar road, with the policy-making establishment quietly saying 'I told you so'.

The real trouble is that this is the middle of the wrong road. If the view is that, whatever the complexion of the Government of the day, for the country to be administered at all a 'deal' must first be done with trade union spokesmen allegedly speaking for a mass working class, then the consent of Parliament is really no more than a formality, and the battle in Parliament largely a charade.

It is the prevailing policy assumptions in British politics which first have to change. The party pattern is secondary. The key question is how Parliament can again become an effective force in reflecting the views of a new majority and a new mood. How can this new mood *get through* to the policy-making level?

It must be done, not through trying to change the inner workings of the parties, not through playing around with the electoral system, certainly not by adding layers of government to the already over-governed regions of the United Kingdom: it has to be done through restoring the involvement and influence of Parliament and its Members in the programmes and policies of the Government machine.

This is a much more popular view than it was. Mounting public pressures on politicians to return to reality are at last beginning to find expression. The change of fashion in economic policy is especially important. While 'deals' with the unions were in fashion there was nothing very serious or detailed for Parliament to do in the economic policy heartland. But once it began to be seen that public expenditure and monetary and fiscal policy were, after all, of central importance, and that 'deals' appeared to be getting us nowhere, then a way began to emerge in which Parliament's role could be restored.

For with the return of public expenditure as an 'issue' it becomes a matter of widespread public concern that every conceivable pressure should be deployed in the critical and open examination of public spending, with a view to securing new priorities and better overall control. The taxpayer, so long in the wilderness, with no say at all in the world of 'social contracts' and deals with the unions, again becomes a crucial political figure.

In this new context, Parliament and its committees at last have a much more serious role to play. The 'deal' has to be with the electorate, and with a variety of interests so widespread and varied that there is no single group or body outside Parliament which can have prior claim to the Executive's ear. Thus Parliament's role becomes much more intimately connected with the success or failure of the policy being pursued by Government. What the 'workers' are alleged to 'want' by those who have an increasingly questionable title to speak for them matters less. What the electors do want matters more.

Stronger Parliamentary all-party committees can undoubtedly play this role. They may have little or nothing to say on behalf of working class solidarity. But, properly run, they can have a great deal to say about taxpayers' interests and government programmes. To me, one of the most reassuring signs that the Conservative Party has begun to understand the new mood is its strong official support for greater Parliamentary control through stronger all-party select committees, and also its interest in making the Comptroller and Auditor General (together with his staff) a servant of Parliament in practice as well as in form. This is a firm response to a new political reality, that policy should be determined and shaped not by the great corporate bodies outside Parliament, but inside Parliament on the anvil of endless debate, questioning and inquiring.

Some committees may not say their piece very well. Their final reports may be poor. But the very process of hearings, evidence published and the preparation and publication of papers by witnesses creates a stream of 'opinion', playing upon the minds of policy-makers in the Executive to decisive effect.

We have now reached the stage where the realities of economic and social life can no longer be prevented from breaking through the false casing of class war politics and class war language. The upsurge of interest in Parliament's role in public policy is a welcome response to this new force. New interests are beginning to assert themselves and new policies being demanded, requiring a new kind of continuing 'consent' which Parliament alone can give with authority.

Hardened traditionalists may argue that it only needs a Parliament with a clear majority for the iron rule of the Whips to be reasserted, for committees to sink back into deferential impotence and for the Executive to go again about its business unmolested, its flank protected by an obedient Parliamentary majority while it settles down for yet another round of talks with the TUC and another disastrous programme of policy 'concessions' to a phantom interest that has in fact melted away.

I do not believe that things will be this way again. And my reason is that the signs of Parliamentary revival are part of a much deeper change in our society. People wish less and less to be consulted or asked for their consent as a class (mainly through their unions) and more and more to have their say as individuals, through their representatives. The policies of the 1980s will no longer be of the type which must at all costs have the 'consent' of the national trade union bosses or bust. They will be policies which need the constant attention of tax-payers, producers, consumers in their diverse guises, which only the intricate and ceaseless pressures of an elected national Parliament can reflect.

We are not there yet. 'Tripartism' lingers on. There are politicians in all parties who hanker after 'policies based on consent' where consent turns out to mean not bona fide consultation — discussion with all parties including trade unions, but the imprimatur of the highly political people who happen to dominate the political wing of organized labour.

In due season, but only when the present gods have been seen to fail once more, the view of the House of Commons will be heard and will prevail and will underpin a policy truly based on consent.

And this will be for one very good reason − that the House of Commons, for all its inadequacies, is a better and more sensitive device for divining the full spread of national opinion, for securing the lasting consent of the British people and for articulating the policy for which that consent will be forthcoming, than ten TUCs, heaped upon twenty CBIs, and capped with thirty White Papers . . . [3]

Perhaps I was being a little too exuberant when I wrote that. Perhaps it was premature. Perhaps it was unfair to the CBI which was even then struggling to escape from the tripartite charade.

But the whole pattern of events since then has surely confirmed the underlying argument − that there is another Britain struggling to break out into the policy arena, that its character and values are closer to those of the old bourgeois classes, so defeated in Britain, although not elsewhere, than to those ascribed to the British working class, that its voice is not yet being anything like fully heard, but that Parliament offers the only ordered channel through which change is going to come.

CHAPTER 10

Concluding Note

So . . . I feel in regard to this aged
England . . . pressed upon by transitions of trade and
competing populations − I see her not dispirited, not
weak, but well remembering that she has seen dark days
before: − indeed with a kind of instinct that she sees a
little better in a cloudy day, and that, in storm of battle
and calamity, she has a secret vigour and a pulse like a
cannon.

Ralph Waldo Emerson

Since this short book is about current politics, some attempt
should perhaps be made to place it in the left-right spectrum
so beloved of political commentators and yet often so
difficult to match with political attitudes within the parties.

Part of the problem is that it is not a spectrum at all. The
Right in Britain has no coherence and shape in the way that
the Left does and cannot accurately be equated with the
Conservative Party in the way that the Left and the Labour
Party go broadly together. The Conservative Party existed
long before the terms Left and Right were imported into
British political comment from France, as Samuel Brittan has
long since reminded us.[1]

Moreover in their common journalistic usages the political

labels Left and Right have tended to become part of the very disease of over-simplification and polarity in British politics which the whole argument of this book seeks to counteract. So there is a special reason for treating this kind of journalistic shorthand with caution.

Nevertheless, if this is the political language in current use an effort must be made to speak in that language if there is to be connection and communication. Where, then, do the concepts of broad personal ownership, dispersed economic power and mass capitalism fit into the conventional picture?

Obviously these ideas are hostile to collectivism where 'collectivism' is used in its abstract, aggregate political sense, although it would not be right to dissociate my theme from collective endeavour on the family and local community scale. Collective patterns of this *miniature* kind always formed a crucial part of the bourgeois ideal and continue to do so in the societies which are developing from it.

But this is something entirely different in spirit and form from the state collectivism which most parts of the British Labour Party and some of the spokesmen (if not all, and if not the rank and file) of the British trade union movement have so avidly embraced. To this kind of centralist philosophy the mass ownership idea is totally opposed, regarding state ownership as no ownership at all.

So this clearly places the views advanced in this book on the 'right' and on the Conservative side. But to which kind of Conservatism do they really belong? Not I think entirely to the brand of 'market economy' Conservative thinking which is usually and erroneously labelled 'right wing' and which has been an increasingly strong element in Conservative policy in recent years.

The principles of the market economy hold a supremely important place in modern Conservative thought, but do they add up to a programme and do they lead us to any positive views about the vital need to spread ownership far more widely in the interests of social and political stability?

When Ludwig Erhard christened his economic

liberalization programme in West Germany in the 1950s the *social* market economy (*Sozialmarktwirtschaft*) he gave market economics a vital extra dimension and lifted it from the level of economic theory to far-seeing political endeavour.[2] The addition of the word 'social' was more than just a recognition that the modern market economy had to live side by side with a large public sector and substantial welfare programmes. It also proclaimed that social policies to encourage a wide diffusion of capital ownership and to maintain communities based on small enterprise and 'bourgeois' or peasant values would, when necessary, take precedence over market forces in the interests of political and social stability.

The arguments advanced in the preceding chapters have tried to achieve the same balance. Sometimes it seems as though those economists who quite justifiably press the free market case on the Conservative Party imagine that it can be translated, at a stroke, into a political programme which will be respected and will work in a world that longs for security.

They are right to believe that market principles now make a far better starting point for the formulation of policy than the half-way house attitudes which have given us incomes policy *à l'anglaise* and the so-called Industrial Strategy. But they are wrong to assume, where they do, that market economics are enough and that all will settle down in prosperity if entrepreneurial talent is given its head, taxes lowered, and public expenditure constrained.

Over and above this, the Conservative Party must also be able to say something clear and with very broad appeal on the central question of ownership and the spread of wealth. If it cannot, then the collectivists, with their beguiling but false claims to ownership 'by the people' will continue to be identified with democratic advance and the Conservatives with a narrow elite, even though the precise opposite may be the underlying position.

Paradoxically, it is now the class politicians and the enemies of property and of bourgeois values who have the most to lose from change and who resist change most energetically. In this situation the case for property ownership becomes the radical case for change and the scepticism of English conservatism about all radical endeavour a less useful ally than in the past. A spark of scepticism is a crucial ingredient of a healthy political philosophy but is it a strong enough weapon against the entrenched machine guns of socialist theory and collectivist propaganda and the well dug-in and comfortably placed classes which man the rampart?

I would like to see the Conservative Party continue to draw on the best parts of its intellectual past but to add something more – a commitment to policies which recognize the true forces at work in modern British society and which carry our nation forward into the post-socialist age. Let the ideals of the market economy be to the fore. But let us also reach out and bring back to the centre of political understanding, the solid values and robust practicality which in former times served the British people so well, which are there in plenty still and which now provide the foundation for the property-owning democracy that could lie ahead.

As we enter an era of overdue reaction against state socialism, against centralism, against mass manipulation and class labelling, the old ownership ideal, too long excluded from any part of the British political debate, acquires a new life. In a far wider and more imaginative form it could become not the instrument of privilege but the weapon of a deeper democracy, a means to freedom under the law, not for thousands, but for millions.

Whatever the shadows of today, tomorrow will not have a socialist masterclass, it will not have flat commanding tele-screens on every wall, through which the worker class can be controlled, and it will not permit ownership of the means of production, distribution and exchange to be concentrated in the hands of a bureaucratic elite.

This will be so because other ideas will prove more powerful, because social and economic change is taking us away from the collectivist pattern and because the British people will not, when finally challenged, allow it. It is also possible that some of their political leaders may understand the direction society is taking and seek by every exertion to encourage and reinforce this movement away from rule of class by class and towards the coming freedom. The future *will* work. But the politicians, the policy-makers and their advisers, must let it do so.

NOTES

Chapter 1: Introduction

1   Lord Hailsham *The Dilemma of Democracy*, Collins, London, 1978 p.14
2   See 'My kind of socialism' *The Observer*, 23 November 1975
3   R. Emmett Tyrell (ed.) *The Future that Doesn't Work*, Doubleday & Co., New York, 1977

Chapter 2: The Thread

1   'Time to Move On', published by the Conservative Political Centre, Feb. 1976
2   *Department of Employment Gazette*, July 1979
3   I have borrowed this phrase from Robert Skidelsky's marvellous essay 'Is Keynes still relevant?' *Encounter*, April 1979

Chapter 3: The Scene

1   See, for example, the comparative work by T. M. Samuels and P. C. McMahon *Savings as Investment in the UK and West Germany*, published by Wilton House for the Anglo-German Foundation, 1977
2   C. Barnett *The Collapse of British Power*, Eyre Methuen, London, 1972
3   R. Lewis and A. Maude *The English Middle Classes*, Pelican, London, 1953
4   K. Popper *The Open Society and its Enemies*, London, 1945, Vol. II
5   *Financial Times*, 29 November 1978

Chapter 4: The Great Exclusion

1 'The Attack on Inflation', Government White Paper, July
   1975; 'The Attack on Inflation, Second Year, Government
   White Paper, July 1976; 'The Attack on Inflation after 31st
   July 1977', Government White Paper, July 1977; 'Winning
   the Battle against Inflation', Government White Paper,
   July 1978
2 J. M. Keynes *The General Theory of Employment, Interest
   and Money*, London, 1936, Vol. vii, Concluding Notes
3 See, for example, J. Strachey *The Nature of the Capitalist
   Crisis*, London, 1935
4 Ibid.
5 And, in particular from G. D. H. Cole *A History of
   Socialist Thought*, London, 1953-60

Chapter 5: A Business People

1 See J. K. Galbraith *Economics and the Public Purse*,
   André Deutsch, London, 1974
2 Ibid.
3 Ibid.
4 'Review of Monopolies and Mergers Policy: A Consultative
   Document', Cmnd 7198
5 See, for example, Prof. Medlik 'Britain: Workshop or
   Service Centre of the World', Surrey University Lecture,
   1977
6 G. Bannock *Smaller Business in Britain and West
   Germany*, published by Wilton House for the Anglo-
   German Foundation, 1976
7 Small Firms Committee of Enquiry. Report., Cmnd 4811,
   Nov. 1971

Chapter 6: The Turning Point

1 A. Huxley *Brave New World*, Chatto & Windus, London,
   1932

2 G. Orwell *Nineteen-Eighty-Four* Martin, Secker & Warburg, London, 1949

3 See P. Johnson *Enemies of Society*, Weidenfeld & Nicolson, 1977 p.22

Chapter 7: The Unofficial Future

1 See Sir Keith Joseph 'Monetarism is not Enough', Centre for Policy Studies, 1975

2 L. Kelso and M. J. Adler *The Capitalist Manifesto*, Random House, New York, 1958

3 J. M. Keynes *How to Pay for the War*, Macmillan, London, 1940

4 Ibid.

5 L. Kelso and J. Adler *The New Capitalists: A Proposal to Free Economic Growth from the Slavery of Savings*, London, 1976

6 S. Brittan 'The age-old lump of labour fallacy', *Financial Times*, 14 December 1978

7 J. K. Galbraith *Economics and the Public Purse*, André Deutsch, London, 1974

8 See C. A. R. Crosland *The Future of Socialism*, Jonathan Cape, London, 1956

Chapter 8: Measures and Money

1 T. M. Samuels and P. C. McMahon *Savings as Investment in the UK and West Germany*, published by Wilton House for the Anglo-German Foundation, 1970, p.44

2 CDU Party Congress, 1958

3 See Note 1, chapter 8

4 G. Copeman *Employee Share Ownership and Industrial Stability*, Institute of Personnel Management, 1975

5 Ibid.

6 Ibid.

7 Conservative Green Paper. Report of a Working Party on Wider Capital Ownership under the chairmanship of the author. Published by the Conservative Research Department, 1975

8   'Outline of an Economic Strategy for the Next
     Conservative Government', published by the Conservative
     Central Office, October 1977
9   Now done by the present Conservative Government
10   N. Goodison 'The Dallas Lecture' 30 November 1978,
     issued to the press by the Stock Exchange Council
11   First outlined in S. Brittan 'Let the people have the oil
     cash', *Financial Times*, 26 May 1977

Chapter 9: Another Britain

1   'A New Style of Government', Conservative Political
     Centre, May 1970
2   Lord Hailsham *The Dilemma of Democracy*, Collins,
     London, 1978
3   The author in *The Times*, 4 August 1975

Chapter 10: Concluding Note

1   S. Brittan *Left or Right: The Bogus Dilemma*, Secker &
     Warburg, 1968
2   Ludwig Erhard *Prosperity through Competition*, Thames &
     Hudson, 1958

INDEX